North Georgia

milestone
press

almond, nc

VOLUME III · BY JIM PARHAM

Copyright ©1993, 1996, 1999 & 2002 by Jim Parham
4th revised edition 1st printing May 2002

Milestone Press, Inc., P.O. Box 158, Almond, NC 28702
www.milestonepress.com

Book design by Ron Roman/Treehouse Communications
www.treehousecomm.com

Library of Congress Cataloging-in-Publication Data

Parham, Jim.
        Off the beaten track / Jim Parham.—2nd rev. ed.
        p. cm.
        Contents: v. 1. A guide to mountain biking in western North
Carolina, the Smokies
        ISBN 0-9631861-4-0 (v. 1 : alk paper)
        1. All terrain cycling—United States—Guidebooks. 2. United
States—Guidebooks. I. Title.
        GV1045.P37   1997
        796.6'4'0973—dc21   97-26133
                                                            CIP
ISBN 1-889596-13-2 (v. 3 4th rev. ed.: alk paper)

*This publication is sold with the understanding that the author and
publisher assume no legal responsibility for the completeness or accuracy of
the contents of this book, nor for damages incurred while attempting any of
the routes within it. Roads and trails can change with time; some roads and
trails may not be marked by signs; distances may vary with individual
cyclocomputers; and land agency rules and regulations are subject to
interpretation and change. There are risks inherent in the sport of mountain
biking. Maps and text are based on information available at the time of
publication.*

Printed in the United States on recycled paper.

Acknowledgements

Each time this book goes through a revision, different individuals come forward with new trail information or ideas that greatly improve it. I'll do my best here to thank those who have helped on this edition as well as on past ones. I am grateful to all of them.

First, I want to thank the various chapters and individual members of the Southern Off-Road Bicycle Association (SORBA). Many of the trails in this book would not exist without the hard work and dedication of the individuals who make up this organization. On days when they could otherwise be out riding their bikes, volunteer members spend time building and maintaining trails, raising money for trail upkeep, and fostering relationships with public land managers so trails will remain open for cycling. These folks work hard, but they also have a lot of fun. I encourage you to help support SORBA by becoming a member yourself. You'll find a membership application in the back of this book.

I also want to acknowledge the agencies which oversee the public lands on which we ride. The Chattahoochee National Forest, which is very proactive toward mountain bike use, has many designated bike trails and numerous new ones planned for the future; most of the trails in this book lie within its boundaries. Forest Service officials Peach Keller, Larry Thomas and Edwin Dale deserve a special thanks. Other land agencies include the Georgia DNR Wildlife Resources, the Georgia DNR State Parks Division (thanks to Wally Woods at Fort Mountain State Park for adding 30 miles of trails!), the Corps of Engineers, the Chicopee Woods Area Park Commission, and Gainesville College.,

Finally, I am grateful to Tom Sauret, the current president of SORBA, for keeping me updated on new trail developments. For their help with previous editions I am indebted to Mike Palmeri, owner of Cartecay River Bicycle Shop in Ellijay, and William Wood, owner of Woody's Mountain Bikes in Helen. Many trails in this book are just out the back doors of their shops, so if you find yourself nearby, be sure to stop in for the latest trail information, any repairs and gear, or just to say hello.

Contents

NORTHEAST GEORGIA

APPENDIX

Introduction

In the north Georgia mountains, it's easy to see why mountain biking is the fastest-growing recreational activity on this country's public lands. Most any day when the weather's right (which is just about any time of year), people flock to the hills with their bikes. In fact, use has grown considerably in the region since the first edition of this book was published in 1993.

Since then, land managers and the Southern Off-Road Bicycle Association (SORBA) have reacted in a way that could serve as a model for other states to follow. In the Chattahoochee National Forest, several of Georgia's state parks, some of the Department of Natural Resources' wildlife management areas and various other locations, new mountain bike trails have been built, routes have been reblazed and renamed, existing trails are consistently maintained, new trailheads have been established, and parking areas have been added. Many more haven't been built yet, but are flagged and marked for construction over the next few years. This newest edition of Off The Beaten Track Vol. III reflects those changes and additions, while retaining all the best rides from past editions.

It's no wonder so many people love to ride in North Georgia—it's a great place for mountain biking. These mountains are chock full of trails and forest roads that can be linked together for some really exciting rides. In the northwest corner of the state is Pigeon Mountain. Flat on top and almost hollow with caves, this spur off Lookout Mountain has a single track network of over 40 miles. Just below it is the brand new Pinhoti Trail, a long distance trail reaching over 50 miles from Dalton to Rome. To the east, across the Great Valley, are the Cohutta Mountains with their many remote and rugged trails. In and around the towns of Blue Ridge, Ellijay and Dahlonega you'll find the Aska Trail System; Fort Mountain State Park; the popular Bull Mountain area and the brand new Jake Mountain area; Amicalola Falls State Park; and Carters Lake. Farther to the east are Helen and Chicopee Woods. On the eastern boundary are Lake Russell, Tallulah Gorge State Park and the trails of Rabun County.

Good riding is just part of the experience. The mountains themselves are over 230 million years old. Rounded off by time and covered with lush vegetation, from a distance they appear gentle and smooth. Once in their heart, though, you'll find them as rugged as they come—complete with waterfalls, cliffs and gorges. Peaks rise to over 4,000 feet, and on clear days you can see forever. You'll find single track trails that travel through remote valleys, along precipitous mountain ridges and through dense forests. Some are steep, rocky and tortuous; others are smooth, fast and relatively easy. Forest roads snake up the valleys and traverse the highest ridges. Some have gates to keep motor vehicles out, while others are so lightly traveled it's rare to see a car. These are good to ride in wet weather when the trails may be muddy. By linking roads and trails together you can create routes that can be ridden in as little as an hour or take as long as an entire day.

One of the best things about mountain biking in north Georgia is that it is a year-round activity. Although a few winter days can be quite cold, most are not too cold, and snow is rare. Summer days are hot, but once in the shade of the mountains, you'll find riding to be very pleasant. Of course, spring and fall temperatures are almost always perfect.

With the changes of the season comes a change in the type of users you are likely to see while out on the trail. In summer you'll encounter tourists of all kinds. Most come to escape the heat of the Deep South. They may be hiking, fishing, camping, tubing in the creek, or biking like yourself. In the fall, the number of cars driven by "leaf peepers" picks up on the forest roads. Give these vehicles a wide berth, as they tend to be looking up most of the time. Late fall and through the winter is hunting season, so be prepared to see folks with guns in the woods. Several of the rides in this book pass through wildlife management areas, and if a hunt is planned, you'll have to ride somewhere else that day. Otherwise, be sure to wear a bright color such as blaze orange while in the woods. Of course, spring in the north Georgia mountains is always beautiful and a great time to ride.

Whether you're a seasoned expert or a first-time mountain biker, you'll find plenty of routes in this book to choose from. When you're first starting out in a new area, it's best not to overestimate your ability level. To get the most out of every ride, pay close attention to the difficulty rating, time estimates, highlights, total distance and elevation profiles as you make your choice.

That said, I wish you wonderful riding. I think you'll be drawn to these mountains again and again, just as I have been.

J.P.
March, 2002

Using This Guide

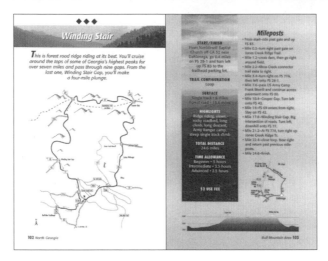

Typical Route Description Pages

- **Route Difficulty** is marked by a series of black diamonds above the route name on the left-hand page. One diamond represents the easiest, while five represents the most difficult of rides. I've rated ride difficulty relative to other routes in this book, and the topography of the area.

- Below the **Route Name** is a brief description of the route's more noted highlights followed by a map highlighting the ride.

- **Start/Finish** indicates where the route begins and how to get there.

- **Trail Configuration** describes the type of route.

- There are three **Surface** types: single track (sometimes double track), forest road and pavement. This will show how many miles of each surface to expect.

- In the **Highlights** there will be a one or two-word description of things you can expect on the trail. For example: Horse use means you may encounter horses, that the trail will have rutted areas with loose rocks, and that any wet places can be very muddy.

- **Total Distance** shows the number of miles you will travel.

- **Time Allowance** is a rough approximation of the time it will take you to ride the trail with minimal stops, according to your ability level.

• **Mileposts** correspond to the adjoining map. The first milepost is at the Start/Finish and is represented by an $\boxed{S}$ on the map. There is a milepost for every turn or any other place of note, and each is represented by a $\boxed{5.3}$ on the map.

• **Maps** are oriented north, with all roads or trails marked by name or number. All roads, trails, buildings, clearings and other features relevant to the route are shown, as well as the best direction of travel. Some of the routes listed in this book can be linked together for shorter or longer rides. When this is the case, those trails or roads are also shown on the map; however, no mileposts or directions are given for these. Maps are not drawn to scale.

• By looking at the **Elevation Profile**, you can get a pretty good idea where the major hills are on the route, how long they will be, and the degree of steepness. It does not show every short rise or dip in the trail.

Map Key

Described Bike Route..........	⌒	Trail or Road Name..........	Big Oak Trail
Paved Motorroad................	═══	Forest Road Number................	477
Gravel Motorroad................	- - - - -	Start/Finish......................................	$\boxed{S}$
Other Forest Road or Trail..	⌒	Milepost.................................	2.2
Unauthorized Trail...............	_ _ _	Suggested Direction...................	→
Foot Travel Only..................	_ _ _ .	Trailheads..	★

A number of different agencies manage the public lands in north Georgia. The vast majority of public land is part of the Chattahoochee National Forest, but you will also find mountain bike trails in the Department of Natural Resources (DNR) wildlife management areas, along the shores of lakes managed by the Corps of Engineers, in Georgia State Parks and in at least one City Area Park. Each of these agencies has various rules and regulations pertaining to mountain cyclists. Riders coming from other states will quickly notice one theme that runs throughout. That is the "use fee." At more and more trailheads and in the various parks, be prepared to pay a few dollars for the privilege of riding there.

CHATTAHOOCHEE NATIONAL FOREST

The Chattahoochee National Forest welcomes mountain bikers. You'll find the trails, trailheads and roads well marked and in good condition. Bikes are allowed on trails signed and posted for bike use as well as on gated and closed Forest Service roads, unless signed otherwise. Bicycles are not allowed in wilderness areas or on the Appalachian Trail.

WILDLIFE MANAGEMENT AREAS

Many of north Georgia's mountain bike trails located in the National Forest and other lands also cross wildlife management areas. These areas are managed by the Georgia Department of Natural Resources. On some days or during certain hours in hunting season, some or all of a management area may be closed to bicycle use. Hunting seasons occur during late fall and a few weeks in spring. you can find out which trails are closed due to hunting on the SORBA web site at www.sorba.org.

WILDLIFE MANAGEMENT AREAS WITH BIKE TRAILS

• Blue Ridge WMA
  (Bull Mountain area)
• Chattahoochee WMA (Helen area)
• Cohutta WMA (Cohuttas area)
• Crockford-Pigeon WMA
  (Pigeon Mountain area)
• Johns Mountain WMA
  (Pinhoti Trail)
• Rich Mountain WMA (Ellijay area)
• Lake Russell WMA (Ladyslipper)
• Warwoman WMA (Sandy Ford)
• Lake Burton WMA
  (trails near Lake Burton)

GEORGIA STATE PARKS

A number of Georgia's state parks now have designated mountain bike trails. All charge a daily parking fee, and Unicoi and Fort Mountain charge an additional bike riding fee. The basic rule: Stay on the designated bike trails, and no riding after dark.

CORPS OF ENGINEERS

The Corps manages the trails alongside Lake Allatoona and Carters Lake. Stay on designated trails and no riding after dark.

CHICOPEE WOODS

The Chicopee Woods trails in Gainesville are managed by the Chicopee Woods Area Park Commision. You'll want to stay on designated trails, and riding at night is allowed only on formal night ride nights. The trails at the Ag Center are closed to cyclists four or five times a year for archery events. You definitely don't want to ride during these times.

Locator Map

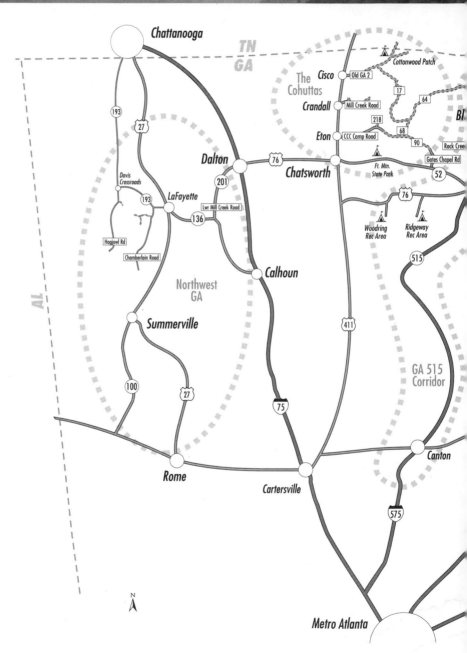

Chattanooga

TN
GA

Cottonwood Patch

Cisco — Old GA 2

The Cohuttas

17

193

Crandall — Mill Creek Road

64

27

218

BI

Eton — CCC Camp Road

68

90

Rock Cree

Dalton

76

Chatsworth

Ft. Mtn.
State Park

Gates Chapel Rd

52

Davis
Crossroads

201

LaFayette

193

Lwr Mill Creek Road

136

76

Woodring
Rec Area

Ridgeway
Rec Area

Hogjowl Rd

Chamberlain Road

Calhoun

515

Northwest
GA

Summerville

411

GA 515
Corridor

100

27

75

Canton

Rome

Cartersville

575

AL

N

Metro Atlanta

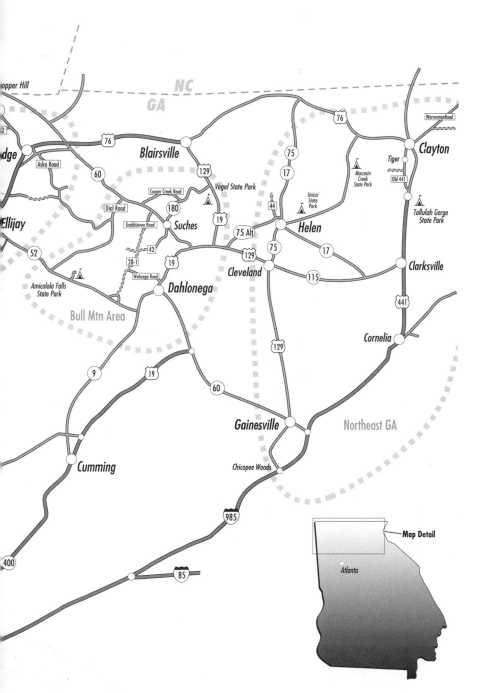

opper Hill

NC
GA

WarwomanRoad

76

76

Blairsville

Tiger

Clayton

Aska Road

75

Moccasin
Creek
State Park

60

129

17

Old 441

Cooper Creek Road

Vogel State Park

Unicoi
State
Park

Tallulah Gorge
State Park

Dial Road

180

44

Ellijay

Gaddistown Road

Suches

19

Helen

52

42

75 Alt

Clarksville

28-1

19

129

75

17

Wahsega Road

Cleveland

115

Amicalola Falls
State Park

Dahlonega

441

Bull Mtn Area

Cornelia

9

19

129

60

Gainesville

Northeast GA

Cumming

Chicopee Woods

985

400

85

Map Detail

Atlanta

Locator Map **13**

Trail Advocacy

When mountain biking first came on the scene in the southeastern United States back in the late 1980s, people could ride their bikes on almost any trail. To see a cyclists on a "foot" trail was a novelty for most people. As the sport took off in the early 1990s, the novelty quickly wore off and the more traditional user groups began claiming turf. Near metropolitan areas where the number of trail users was high, conflicts were inevitable. Threats of those conflicts eventually spread to the remotest portions of the forest as land managers began taking hard looks at what trails were suitable for which user groups.

Now, more than a decade later, mountain bikers have learned a lot of valuable lessons. Bicycle clubs have evolved to include trail advocacy directors and work crews. Some even have thousands of dollars worth of trail building tools. Most every weekend, somewhere in the Southeast there's a group of cyclists out repairing or building a trail. The organization all these folks look to (and most are members of) is the International Mountain Biking Association (IMBA). IMBA's mission is to promote environmentally sound and socially responsible biking. IMBA does everything from sending paid trail crew specialists across the country, to sponsoring trail work camps, to lobbying land managers on the national and international level.

RULES OF THE TRAIL

• **Ride on open trails only**. Respect trail and road closures, and avoid possible trespass on private land. Federal and state wilderness areas are closed to cycling. The way you ride will influence trail management decisions and policies.

• **Leave no trace**. Be sensitive to the dirt beneath you. Many trails in this part of North Carolina can become quite muddy after periods of prolonged rain or freeze-thaw conditions. Consider riding on the hard packed forest roads at these times.

• **Control your bicycle**. Inattention for even a second can cause problems. Don't create danger for yourself and other trail users.

• **Always yield trail**. Make known your approach well in advance. A friendly greeting is considerate and works well; don't startle others. Show your respect when passing by slowing to a walking pace or even stopping. Anticipate meeting other trail users around corners and in blind spots.

• **Never spook animals**. When passing horses, use special care and follow directions from the horseback riders (ask if uncertain). Always ride slowly and quietly through areas where wildlife may be feeding or nesting.

• **Plan ahead**. Know your equipment, your ability and the area in which you are riding—and prepare accordingly. Always wear a helmet.

MORE INFORMATION

For more information or to join any of these trail advocacy groups, contact below:

• **IMBA**
P.O. Box 7578
Boulder, CO 80306
303-545-9011
www.imba.org

• **SORBA**
P.O. Box 1358
Gainesville, GA 30503
770-718-3674
www.sorba.org

Northwest Georgia

Seperated from the rest of the north Georgia mountains by the Great Valley, northwest Georgia's hills are markedly different from those to the east. The Lookout Mountain plateau stretches its southern end into Georgia and from it extends Pigeon Mountain, sticking out like a thumb. True to the plateau character, it's relatively flat on top and drops straight off on either side. This phenomenon provides for some very interesting scenery. Along the rim of the plateau are sheer cliffs with stunning views. On clear days you can see all the way across the Great Valley to Fort Mountain and the Cohuttas.

Mountain biking on Pigeon Mountain is also different than in the rest of the state. If you start on top of the plateau you'll find there are no major climbs, but whenever you cross from one side of a creek drainage to another it's pretty much an abrupt, up-down affair. Most of the rock is limestone, and water eats away at it pretty quickly. Creeks eat away at the top of the mountain, and at its insides as well. Pigeon mountain is full of caves.

Just east of the Lookout Plateau, a few mountains roll out like sharp-pointed waves. Along the top of Taylors Ridge, Horn, and Rocky Face Mountains rolls the long Pinhoti Trail. This trail, when completed (it begins in Alabama), will connect to the Appalachian Trail. Unlike the AT, you can ride a (continues)

Northwest Georgia

mountain bike on much of its length. Whichever section of this trail you choose, you're in for quite a ride. The northern portion is very rocky and as challenging a ride as any in the state. The southern stretch just seems to go on forever.

The Simms Mountain Trail, a section of Pinhoti that is actually a rail-trail, is so easy it will delight any cyclist. You'll find it down near Rome.

Pigeon Mountain
High Point
North Pocket
Pinhote North
Pinhote South
Simms Mountain

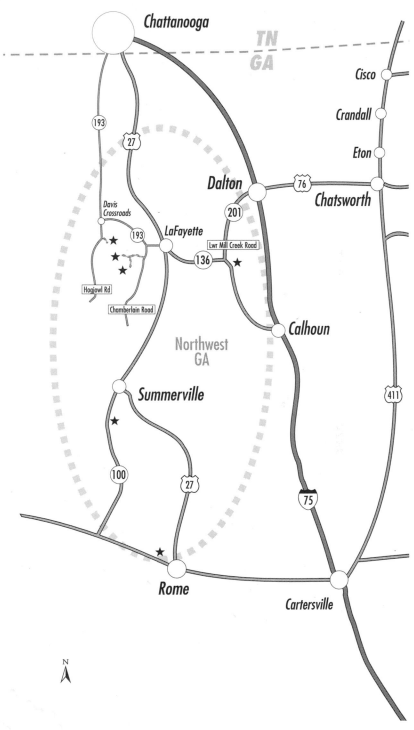

Chattanooga

TN
GA

Cisco

Crandall

Eton

193

27

Dalton

76

Chatsworth

Davis
Crossroads

201

LaFayette

193

Lwr Mill Creek Road

136

Hogjowl Rd

Chamberlain Road

Northwest
GA

Calhoun

Summerville

411

100

27

75

Rome

Cartersville

N

Pigeon Mountain

Pigeon Mountain has many cliffs and caves, and is laced with trails. This route explores its high plateau, which offers excellent cliff-top views, rolling terrain and many small stream crossings. Expect several short sections that are rocky, steep, and difficult to ride.

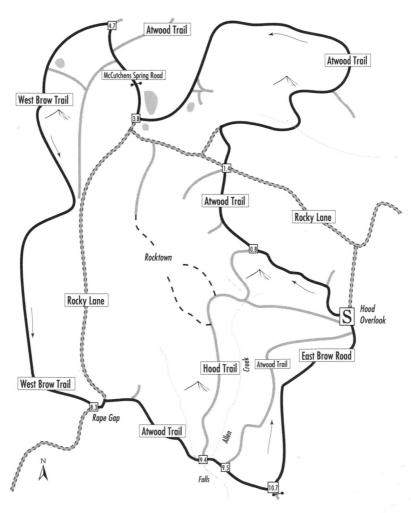

START/FINISH

From LaFayette, take GA 193 north 2.8 miles and turn left on Chamberlain Road. Go 3.5 miles and turn right on Rocky Ln. Continue past the check station up the mountain 3.6 miles and turn left on East Brow Rd. Go 0.25 miles to Hood Overlook to start.

TRAIL CONFIGURATION
Loop

SURFACE
Single track • 8.7 miles
Forest road • 3.7 miles

HIGHLIGHTS
Spectacular views; horse use; stream crossings; short, steep rocky sections; many unmarked side trails

TOTAL DISTANCE
12.4 miles

TIME ALLOWANCE
Beginner • 4 hours
Intermediate • 3 hours
Advanced • 2 hours

Mileposts

- From start–follow orange-blazed Atwood Trail into field away from overlook.
- Mile 0.8–Hood Trail enters from left. Bear right.
- Mile 1.4–cross Rocky Lane.
- Mile 3.8– turn right on McCutchens Spring Road.
- Mile 4.7–turn left onto West Brow Trail (white blaze).
- Mile 8.3–Rape Gap. Turn left on Rocky Lane, go a few hundred yards, then right on Atwood Trail (orange blaze).
- Mile 9.4–Hood Trail exits left. Cross Allen Creek.
- Mile 9.5–Atwood Trail exits left. Waterfall to right. Continue straight over dirt mound onto jeep road.
- Mile 10.7–bear left onto East Brow Road.
- Mile 12.4–finish.

West Brow

cross Allen Cr

2000'

1000'

High Point

This route explores the rolling midsection of Pigeon Mountain before making the rocky climb to High Point and a spectacular cliff-top view. The ride down is across giant slabs of stone, through the woods, and along the rim of the mountain.

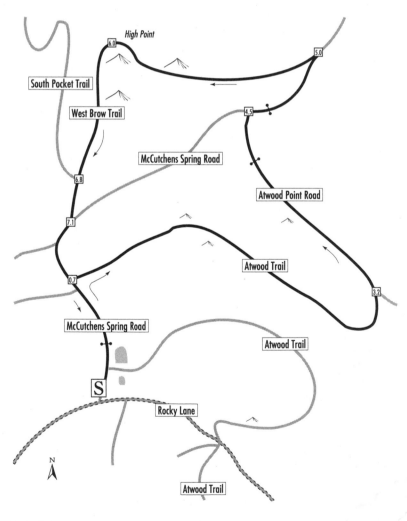

START/FINISH

From LaFayette, take GA 193 north 2.8 miles and turn left on Chamberlain Road. Go 3.5 miles and turn right on Rocky Lane. Continue past the check station up the mountain 5 miles and turn right on McCutchens Spring Road. Start at campsite.

TRAIL CONFIGURATION
Loop w/ extension

SURFACE
Single track • 5 miles
Forest road • 3.3 miles

HIGHLIGHTS
Spectacular views, horse use, steep climb, boulders and rock slabs, short pushes

TOTAL DISTANCE
8.3 miles

TIME ALLOWANCE
Beginner • 4 hours
Intermediate • 2.5 hours
Advanced • 1.5 hours

Mileposts

- From start–ride down McCutchens Spring Road out past ponds and around gate.
- Mile 0.7–turn right on Atwood Trail (orange blaze).
- Mile 3.2–turn left onto Atwood Point Road.
- Mile 4.5–turn right onto McCutchens Spring Road and continue down and around gate.
- Mile 5–turn left onto West Brow Trail (blue and white double blazes). Start hill climb.
- Mile 6.0–High Point.
- Mile 6.8–South Pocket Trail exits right.
- Mile 7.1–turn right onto McCutchens Spring Road and continue on it to the finish.
- Mile 8.3–finish.

◆ ◆ ◆ ◆

North Pocket

Don't be discouraged by the first bit of trail, which is steep and washed out. Soon you'll find great curving single track that skirts a series of abandoned mine tunnels. The climb up to the top of the Pocket is rocky, demanding and sometimes impossible, while the return to the bottom is a challenge in itself.

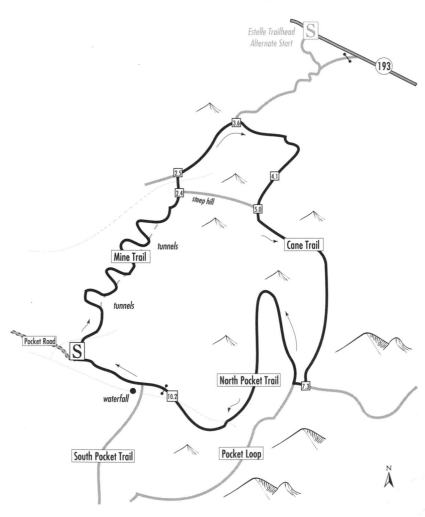

START/FINISH

Take GA 193 west of LaFayette 8 miles to Davis Crossroads and turn left onto Hogjowl Road. Go 2.7 miles and turn left onto Pocket Road. It's 1.3 more miles to the trailhead.

TRAIL CONFIGURATION

Loop

SURFACE

Single track • 9.3 miles
Forest road • 1.6 miles

HIGHLIGHTS

Tunnels, views, stream crossings, severe washouts, horse use, very rocky climb, big waterfall

TOTAL DISTANCE

10.9 miles

TIME ALLOWANCE

Beginner • not advised
Intermediate • 4.5 hours
Advanced • 3 hours

Mileposts

- From start–ride out back of trailhead parking across creek onto orange-blazed Mine Trail. Within the first mile you should start to see tunnel entrances.
- Mile 2.4–trail exits right. Stay on Mine Trail.
- Mile 2.5–cross creek and turn right onto forest road.
- Mile 3.6–bear right and start following white blazes of Cane Trail up the road.
- Mile 4.1–road ends. Trail begins. This is the beginning of the tough, rocky climbing section.
- Mile 5.0–a trail exits to the right. Stay on Cane Trail.
- Mile 7.3–end of difficult climb. Turn right and then right again onto blue-blazed North Pocket Trail.
- Mile 10.2–continue onto forest road and past gate.
- Mile 10.9–finish.

Pinhote North

*Y*ou'll need to have your fillings checked after this one. It's got to be the rockiest trail in north Georgia and if it doesn't beat you to death, you'll love it. There are some awesome views if you're brave enough to take your eyes from the trail.

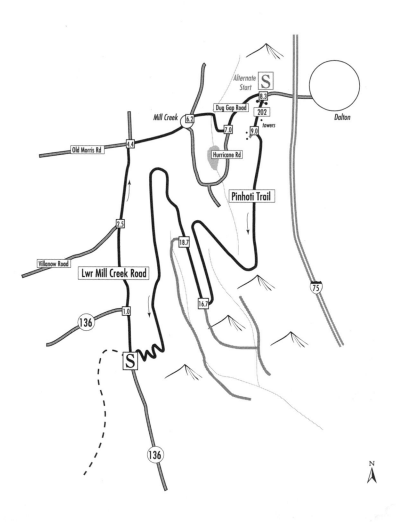

START/FINISH
Pinhoti trailhead parking on GA 136, five miles north of Resaca. *Alternate start: Dug Gap, between Dalton and Mill Creek.*

TRAIL CONFIGURATION
Loop or Point-to-Point (to avoid paved road and climb)

SURFACE
Single track • 13.3 miles
Forest road • 2.6 miles
Pavement • 8.3

HIGHLIGHTS
2-mile climb to trail, rocks and boulders, views, very technical

TOTAL DISTANCE
24.2 miles

TIME ALLOWANCE
Beginner • not advised
Intermediate • 5 hours
Advanced • 4 hours

Mileposts
- From start–ride north on GA 136.
- Mile 1.0–turn right on Lower Mill Creek Road.
- Mile 2.5–Villanow Road enters from left. Bear right.
- Mile 4.4–turn right on Old Morris Road.
- Mile 6.2–Mill Creek. Turn right on Hurricane Road.
- Mile 7–bear left on Dug Gap Road and start climb.
- Mile 8.3–Dug Gap. Turn right on FS 202.
- Mile 9.0–turn left on Pinhoti Trail (white blaze or white plastic diamond) at second set of towers.
- Mile 16.7–turn right on forest road.
- Mile 18.7–turn right on old woods road.
- Mile 24.2–finish.

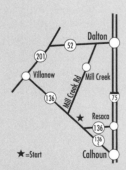

★ =Start

Dug Gap

1000'

*T*his difficult ride is best done as a point-to-point by leaving a car at either end. It's long and it throws the book at you—everything from fast single track, arduous climbs, and old forest roads to deep gravel, amazing views, briars, and sticker bushes.

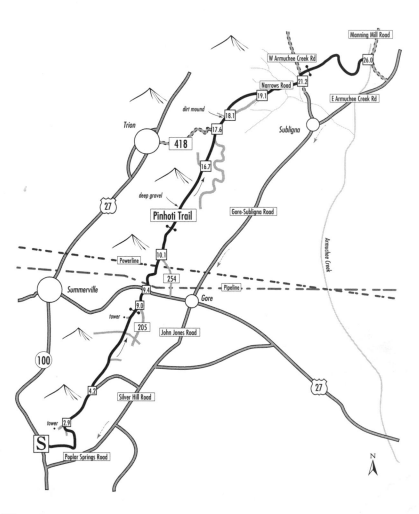

START/FINISH

Pinhoti Trailhead parking, 4 miles south of Summerville on GA 100. Finish: 1 mile up Manning Mill Road off East Armuchee Creek Road, 3.6 miles north of Subligna.

TRAIL CONFIGURATION

Point-to-Point

SURFACE

Single track • 17.6 miles
Forest road • 6.4 miles
Pavement • 2 miles

HIGHLIGHTS

Rocky climb, lots of short ups and downs, ridgetop riding, views, horse use

TOTAL DISTANCE

26 miles

TIME ALLOWANCE

Beginner • not advised
Intermediate • 6 hours
Advanced • 4.5 hours

Mileposts

- From start–ride out of parking and up hill on Pinhoti Trail (white blaze).
- Mile 2.9–bear right on roadway.
- Mile 4.2–turn left off road onto single track.
- Mile 9.0–turn left past gate on FS 205.
- Mile 9.4–cross US 27 and bear left up hill.
- Mile 10.1–turn left on FS 254.
- Mile 16.7–turn right on road.
- Mile 17.6–bear right on Narrows Road.
- Mile 18.1–turn right onto single track.
- Mile 19.1–trailhead. Bear left on Narrows Road.
- Mile 21.2–turn left on West Armuchee Creek Road, then turn right up past gate on Pinhoti Trail.
- Mile 26.0–finish.

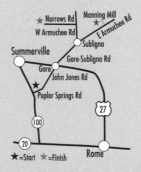

cross US 27

gain ridgetop

1000'

Simms Mountain

***A** pleasant ride through the northwest Georgia country-side, this rail-trail is flat as a pancake. It connects with the Pinhoti South ride at its northern terminus and is part of the much longer Pinhoti Trail. There's not much shade, so be prepared for that on a hot summer day.*

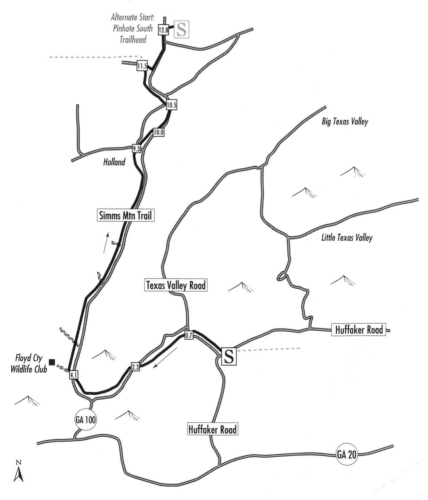

Alternate Start:
Pinhote South
Trailhead
12.8

11.5

10.5

Big Texas Valley

10.0

9.3

Holland

Simms Mtn Trail

Little Texas Valley

Texas Valley Road

Huffaker Road

0.7

Floyd Cty
Wildlife Club
2.3

4.1

GA 100

Huffaker Road

GA 20

N

START/FINISH

Get on the Connector at Berry College in Rome and then turn right on Technology Drive which becomes Huffaker Rd. The trail starts just east of Big Texas Valley Rd. There's limited parking beside the road.
Aternate start: Pinhoti South trailhead.

TRAIL CONFIGURATION

Point-to-Point or Out and Back

SURFACE

Rail-trail • 12.8 miles (one way)

HIGHLIGHTS

Horse use, ATV use (although it's not allowed) flat surface, big gravel in places

TOTAL DISTANCE

12.8 miles (one way)

TIME ALLOWANCE

Beginner • 2.5 hours
Intermediate • 1.5 hours
Advanced • 1+ hours

Mileposts

- From start–ride onto rail-trail.
- Mile 0.7–cross Big Texas Valley Road (there's more parking here).
- Mile 2.3–cross paved road.
- Mile 4.1–cross GA 100 and bear right to continue on rail-trail.
- Mile 9.3–pass through community of Holland. This is a good place to turn around if you are doing an out and back ride.
- Mile 10.0–the rail-trail temporarily ends where no right-of-way was given across private land. You'll need to follow the highway here for half a mile.
- Mile 10.5–turn left on Worsham Road, then right to pick up the rail-trail again.
- Mile 11.5–the rail-trail only continues a short way from here before stopping at a chain-link fence. Turn right on roadway and then left on GA 100 to continue to the Pinhoti trailhead.
- Mile 12.8–finish at Pinhoti Trailhead.

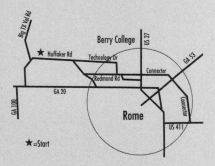

The Cohuttas

If you really want to head out into the boonies, the place to go is the Cohutta Mountains. This mountain range which lies on the eastern side of the Great Valley contains some of the remotest backcountry in north Georgia. In the heart of the Cohuttas is the Cohutta Wilderness, where only foot traffic is allowed and even the trails are barely marked. If you are in the area for a while and want a break from your bike, take a hike here for a real "off the beaten track" experience. The bulk of the mountain biking opportunities lie around the edges of this wilderness.

Up near the Tennessee border you'll find a number of nice rides. These routes alongside the Conasauga River, over Iron Mountain, and around Sumac Creek require long drives on rocky dirt roads just to get to the trailheads. Once there, you'll find some awesome trails built with mountain biking in mind. Just remember the Iron Mountain ride is dry and the other two will get you wet, so plan your trips there during warmer weather.

Another hot location for mountain cyclists is the Bear Creek area. Riders here will find a nice camping spot, pretty waterfalls just off the road, and one of Georgia's largest trees. The riding is spectacular here as well. Stick close to Bear Creek or head out onto the very remote Mountaintown Creek Trail.

(continues)

The Cohuttas

Also in the region are a few routes you'll share with ORVs, ATVs, and motorcycles. This does not mean you'll always see them on the trail, but keep in mind these trails were also built for their specific use. Stick to the ORV areas for the easier rides and expect difficult conditions if you see ATV or motorcycle listed on the signpost. Remember, those guys have gas powered engines for getting up steep hills.

Fort Mountain is not technically in the Cohuttas, but it overlooks them. It gets its name from a jumble of rocks atop the mountain which some speculate is the ruins of an ancient fort. You can read all about this while in the Park. In addition to the old rock jumble, the State Park has a campground, cabins, a lake, a lookout tower, and observation decks. Most importantly, though, you'll find trails which were specifically built for mountain bike use. You can choose anything from an easy spin around the lake to an exhilarating lung buster of a ride around the entire mountain.

Conasauga River
Iron Mountain
Sumac Creek
Rocky Flats
Windy Gap
Bear Creek
Mountaintown Creek
Tatum Lead
Fort Mountain Lake
Gold Mine
Cool Springs
East West

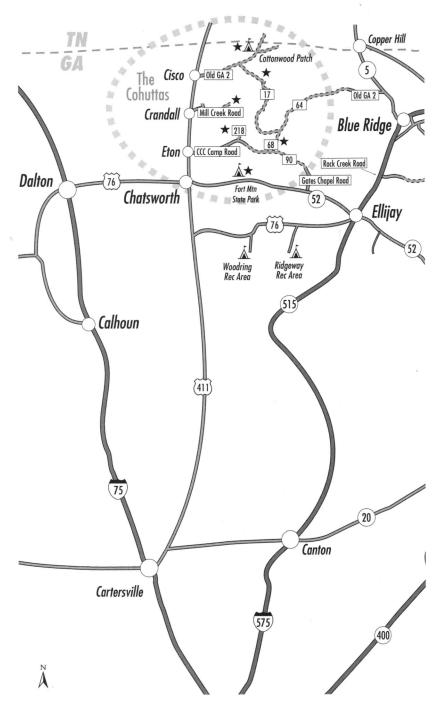

Conasauga River

*Y*ou definitely should do this ride only if the weather is warm, as you'll cross the river twice and the second crossing is long and deep. Beautiful views await you, along with the river and a fun section of whoop-te-doos. Plan on getting wet—really wet.

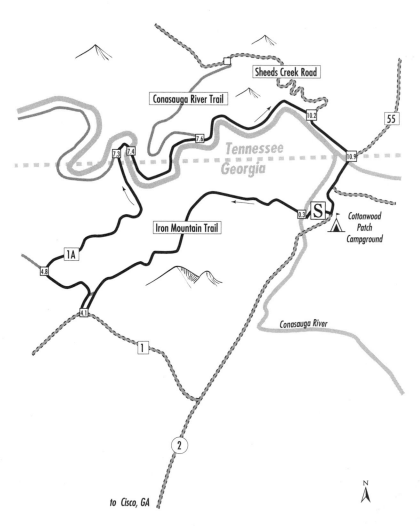

START/FINISH
From Cisco, on US 411, take Old GA 2 eight miles to Cottonwood Patch Campground to start.

TRAIL CONFIGURATION
Loop

SURFACE
Single track • 7.3 miles
Forest road • 4.4 miles

HIGHLIGHTS
Spectacular views, horse use, deep river crossing, whoop-te-doos, old rail grade

TOTAL DISTANCE
11.7 miles

TIME ALLOWANCE
Beginner • 4 hours
Intermediate • 3 hours
Advanced • 2 hours

$2 USE FEE

Mileposts

- From start–ride out back of campground.
- Mile 0.3–ford the Conasauga River.
- Mile 4.1–turn right onto FS 1 and then immediately right again on FS 1A.
- Mile 4.8–bear right at road fork.
- Mile 7.3–turn hard right onto old roadbed.
- Mile 7.4–steep downhill followed by river crossing.
- Mile 7.6–Conasauga River Trail enters from left.
- Mile 10.2–trailhead. Continue onto Sheeds Creek Road.
- Mile 10.9–turn right and cross bridge.
- Mile 11.7–finish at campground.

Warning: do not attempt this ride after heavy rains or if the river appears to be swollen. You could easily be swept away on the second river crossing.

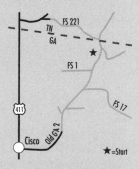

Iron Mtn Tr

river crossing

1000'

Iron Mountain

*T*he single track portion of this trail twists and winds along the side of Iron Mountain while a forest road takes you to an old tower site with spectacular views. If the river is up, be sure to take the alternate high-water route at the beginning to avoid being swept away.

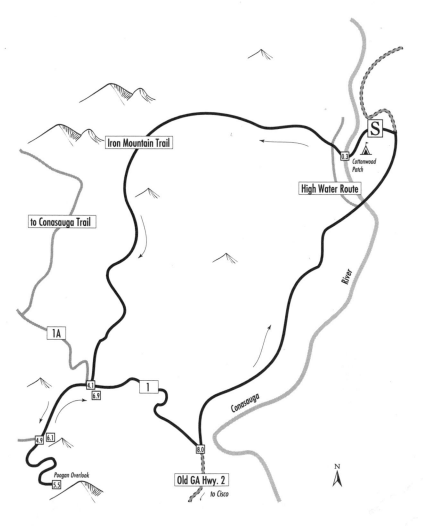

Iron Mountain Trail

S

0.3 Cottonwood Patch

High Water Route

to Conasauga Trail

River

1A

4.1
6.9

1

4.9 6.1

Conasauga

8.0

Poogan Overlook
5.5

Old GA Hwy. 2
to Cisco

N

START/FINISH
From Cisco, on US 411, take Old GA 2 eight miles to Cottonwood Patch Campground to start.

TRAIL CONFIGURATION
Loop w/extension

SURFACE
Single track • 4.1 miles
Forest road • 6.9 miles

HIGHLIGHTS
Spectacular view, horse use, river crossing, twisty single track

TOTAL DISTANCE
11 miles

TIME ALLOWANCE
Beginner • 2.5 hours
Intermediate • 1.5 hours
Advanced • 1 hour

$2 USE FEE

Mileposts

- From start–ride along river and out back of campground.
  Alternate start: If the river is running high, go back the way you drove in, cross the bridge, turn right on the forest road and ride downstream to the river crossing.
- Mile 0.3–ford the Conasauga River.
- Mile 4.1–turn right onto FS 1.
- Mile 4.9–road exits right, bear left.
- Mile 5.5–old lookout site. Turn around.
- Mile 6.1–pass road exiting to left.
- Mile 6.9–pass entrance to Iron Mountain Trail.
- Mile 8–turn left onto Old GA 2.
- Mile 11–finish.

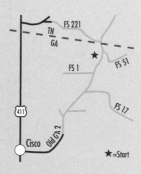

★=Start

Overlook

Iron Mtn Tr

2000'

1000'

Sumac Creek

*T*his remote ride offers a good bit of everything. You'll find smooth single track, double track, whoop-te-doos, tight switchbacks, stream crossings, forest roads, views, and even a bailout route. It's likely you'll see few people, as getting to the trailhead is a bit rougher than the ride itself.

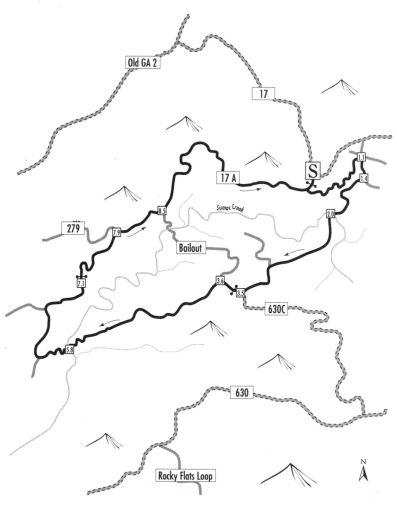

START/FINISH

From Cisco, on US 411, take Old GA 2 three miles and turn right on FS 17. Go 2.1 bumpy miles to the trailhead parking area.

TRAIL CONFIGURATION

Loop

SURFACE

Single/double track • 7.1 miles
Forest road • 3.6 miles

HIGHLIGHTS

Views, horse use, stream crossings, switchbacks, whoop-te-doos, fast descents

TOTAL DISTANCE

10.7 miles

TIME ALLOWANCE

Beginner • 3 hours
Intermediate • 2 hours
Advanced • 1.75 hours

Mileposts

- From start–ride out FS 17A and then left onto trail.
- Mile 1.1–take far right at 5-way jct. on double track.
- Mile 1.4–bear right at fork.
- Mile 2.0–cross stream.
- Mile 3.5–jct. end of FS 630. Go around gate, turn right and go around another gate.
- Mile 3.6–had enough? Bail out right. Bear left for loop.
- Mile 5.8–2nd stream crossing, then very steep climb.
- Mile 7.1–go around gate and continue on FS 17A.
- Mile 7.9–FS 279 enters from left.
- Mile 8.5–bailout reenters from right.
- Mile 10.7–finish.

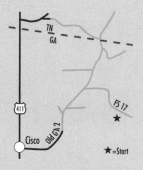

★=Start

1st stream crossing   2nd stream crossing

1000'

Rocky Flats

An easy ride with relatively few hills and lots of views of the surrounding mountains. Be ready for one really fast downhill with numerous large whoop-te-doos near the end of the loop.

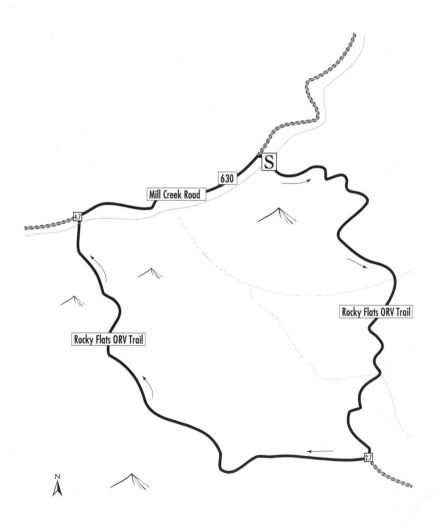

START/FINISH
From Crandall, GA, go east 4 miles on Mill Creek Road (FS 630), to the second Rocky Flats ORV sign.

TRAIL CONFIGURATION
Loop

SURFACE
Double track • 4.7 miles
Forest road • 1.1 miles

HIGHLIGHTS
ORV and ATV use, wildlife openings, timber cuts, whoops, stream crossing

TOTAL DISTANCE
5.8 miles

TIME ALLOWANCE
Beginner • 1 hour
Intermediate • 45 mins
Advanced • 35 minutes

Mileposts
- From start–ride out ORV trail away from Mill Creek Road.
- Mile 2.7–road forks. Bear right on main road.
- Mile 4.7–steep downhill to stream crossing. Bear left up the hill after crossing the stream, then turn right onto Mill Creek Road.
- Mile 5.8–finish.

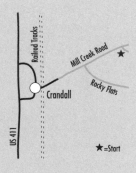

Railroad Tracks

Mill Creek Road ★

Rocky Flats

Crandall

US 411

★ =Start

Rocky Flats

Stream Crossing

1000'

Windy Gap

First, you'll take to the side of Grassy Mountain on the technical Milma Trail before making the long steep climb up Tibbs Trail to the highest point near Lake Conasauga. Then, hold onto your socks! The descent is steep, rocky, difficult, and a real blast.

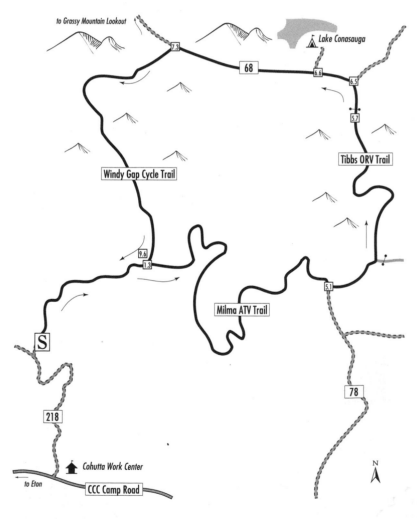

to Grassy Mountain Lookout

Lake Conasauga

7.3

68

6.6

6.5

5.7

Tibbs ORV Trail

Windy Gap Cycle Trail

9.6

1.3

5.1

Milma ATV Trail

S

78

218

Cohutta Work Center

to Eton

CCC Camp Road

N

Mileposts

- From start–ride up Windy Gap Cycle Trail.
- Mile 1.3–begin loop by turning right onto Milma ATV Trail.
- Mile 5.1–turn left up Tibbs ORV Trail.
- Mile 5.7–continue past gate.
- Mile 6.5–turn left onto FS 68.
- Mile 6.6–bear left at fork. The right fork goes to Lake Conasauga Recreation Area.
- Mile 7.3–turn left down Windy Gap Cycle Trail.
- Mile 9.6–Milma Trail enters from left. Continue straight on Windy Gap Cycle Trail back to trailhead.
- Mile 10.9–finish.

START/FINISH
From the stoplight in Eton, go east on CCC Camp Road 4.3 miles. Turn left on FS 218. It's 2 miles to the trailhead.

TRAIL CONFIGURATION
Loop w/extension

SURFACE
Single track • 8.7 miles
Forest road • 2.2 miles

HIGHLIGHTS
Views, ORV and ATV use, steep climb, very technical downhill, banked turns

TOTAL DISTANCE
10.9 miles

TIME ALLOWANCE
Beginner • 4 hours
Intermediate • 3 hours
Advanced • 2 hours

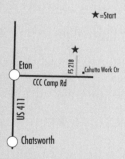

★=Start

Eton
FS 218
Cohutta Work Ctr
CCC Camp Rd
US 411
Chatsworth

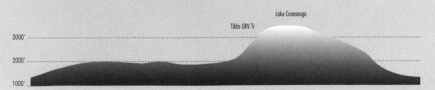

Lake Conasauga
Tibbs ORV Tr
3000'
2000'
1000'

Bear Creek

The single track on this trail is just technical enough to test your skills, and riding across and alongside the stream is beautiful. You'll also pass the immense Gennett Poplar.

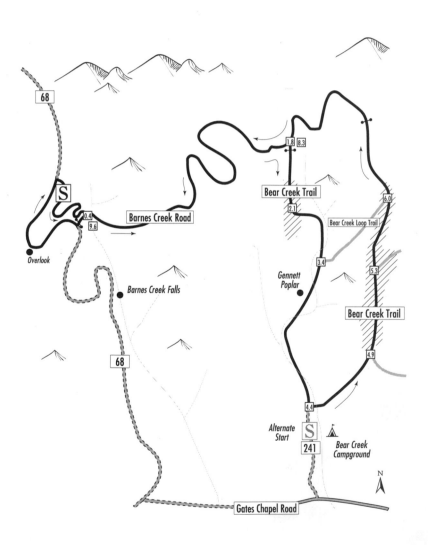

START/FINISH

From milepost 8 on GA 52 west of Ellijay, take Gates Chapel Rd. 5.4 miles. Continue onto FS 90 for another 1.7 miles, turn right on FS 68 and go 2 miles to the bicycle trailhead parking area.

TRAIL CONFIGURATION

Loop w/extension

SURFACE

Single/double track • 9.6 miles
Forest road • 0.5 miles

HIGHLIGHTS

Woods roads, whoops, great views, stream crossings, Gennett Poplar, one very steep uphill, wildlife openings

TOTAL DISTANCE

10.1 miles

TIME ALLOWANCE

Beginner • 2.25 hours
Intermediate • 1.5 hours
Advanced • 1.25 hours

$2 USE FEE

Mileposts

- From start–ride out back of parking area onto trail.
- Mile 0.4–turn left onto Barnes Creek Road.
- Mile 1.8–turn right past gate onto Bear Creek Trail.
- Mile 2.1–at wildlife opening, turn left over whoop-te-doo.
- Mile 3.4–Bear Creek Loop sign marks trail to left. Continue straight down the creek past Gennett Poplar.
- Mile 4.4–lower trailhead. Go 200 feet and trail continues on left side of road. Look for the blue blazes.
- Mile 4.9–turn left onto grassy roadbed.
- Mile 5.3–go left at fork following blue-blazed posts.
- Mile 6.0–Bear Creek Loop Trail exits left. Stay right.
- Mile 8.3–pass Bear Creek Trail sign on left.
- Mile 9.6–pass trail to parking lot, then turn right past gate onto FS 68.
- Mile 10.1–finish.

Mountaintown Creek

This is one of the most remote rides in North Georgia. You'll climb to the ridgeline bordering the Cohutta Wilderness before dropping down into the Mountaintown Creek Gorge with its many cascades and waterfalls. It's then a short ride through the valley before the long climb back to the trailhead.

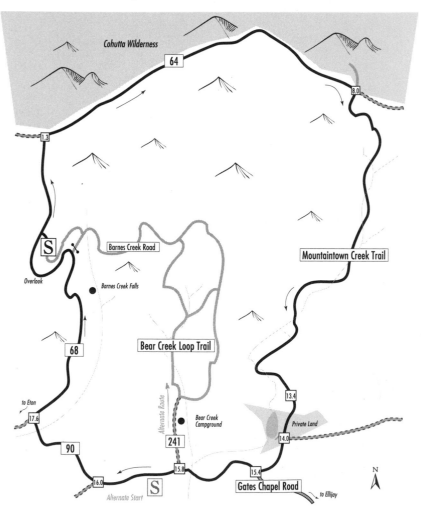

START/FINISH
From milepost 8 on GA 52 west of Ellijay, take Gates Chapel Rd. 5.4 miles. Continue onto FS 90 for another 1.7 miles, turn right on FS 68 and go 2 miles to the bicycle trailhead parking area.

TRAIL CONFIGURATION
Loop

SURFACE
Single track • 5.4 miles
Forest road • 13.6 miles
Pavement • 0.6 miles

HIGHLIGHTS
Remote, views, cascades and waterfalls, multiple stream crossings, boggy areas, long climb, mountain farms

TOTAL DISTANCE
19.6 miles

TIME ALLOWANCE
Beginner • 5 hours
Intermediate • 3.25 hrs
Advanced • 2.5 hours

$2 USE FEE

Mileposts

- From start–ride uphill on FS 68.
- Mile 1.3–turn right onto FS 64.
- Mile 8.0–turn right onto Mountaintown Creek Trail.
- Mile 13.4–lower trailhead for Mountaintown Creek Trail.
- Mile 14.0–pass pond on right. A road enters on the right and a little farther on a road enters on the left. Stay straight.
- Mile 15.4–turn right onto paved Gates Chapel Road.
- Mile 15.8–for an alternate return via the Bear Creek Loop Trail, turn right here on FS 241. Otherwise, go straight.
- Mile 16.0–turn right onto gravel road which is FS 90.
- Mile 17.6–turn right onto FS 68.
- Mile 19.6–finish.

Tatum Lead

A *real teeth-rattler at times, this route follows the ridgeline of Tatum Mountain out and back. The steep, whoop-te-doo-filled side loop on the far end will definitely get your attention.*

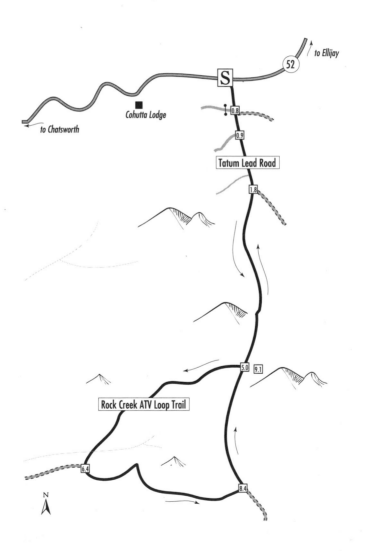

to Ellijay

52

S

0.8

Cohutta Lodge

to Chatsworth

0.9

Tatum Lead Road

1.8

5.0 9.1

Rock Creek ATV Loop Trail

6.4

8.4

N

START/FINISH
One mile east of Cohutta Lodge on GA 52 at the entrance to Tatum Lead Road. *There is very limited parking here, so you may want to ask permission and park at the lodge.*

TRAIL CONFIGURATION
Lollipop

SURFACE
Single/double track • 7.3 miles
Forest Road • 7.2 miles

HIGHLIGHTS
Steep uphill and downhill, rocky trail, whoop-te-doos, spotty views, ATV and ORV use

TOTAL DISTANCE
14.5 miles

TIME ALLOWANCE
Beginner • 3.5 hours
Intermediate • 2.5 hours
Advanced • 1.75 hours

MILEPOSTS
- From start–ride south on Tatum Lead Road. This road starts out as a right of way across private land.
- Mile 0.8–you'll pass a gated road on the right and a little farther along, another road on the left. Continue straight on at each junction.
- Mile 0.9–a road goes downhill to the right. Stay left.
- Mile 1.8–Forest Service boundary. Just past where a jeep road turns off to the left, the road forks. Go right.
- Mile 5.0–turn right onto Rock Creek ATV Loop Trail.
- Mile 6.4–turn left (uphill) at ATV loop sign.
- Mile 8.4–turn left back onto Tatum Lead Road.
- Mile 9.1–pass turnoff to Rock Creek ATV Loop Trail.
- Mile 14.5–continue past previous mileposts to finish.

★=Start

Cohutta Lodge

Fort Mountain State Park •

Chatsworth
GA 52

Ellijay

US 411

GA 5/515

bottom of ATV Loop

2000'

1000'

Fort Mountain Lake

*T*his short loop around the lake at Fort Mountain State Park is as easy to follow as it gets. The trail follows the edge of the lake the entire way. This is not a ride for high speeds, but more of a beginner loop where folks can get used to single track riding before venturing onto the Park's more difficult trails. Some people make it an addition to the Gold Mine Loop. It's great for kids!

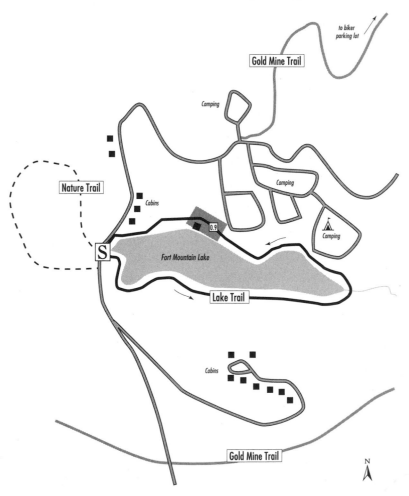

MILEPOSTS
- From start–on the far side of the dam, take the green-blazed Lake Trail counter-clockwise around the lake. Keep on the lookout for walkers, fishermen, etc.
- Mile 0.9–cross through swimming area parking lot and return to trail on the far side .
- Mile 1.2–finish.

START/FINISH
Anywhere within Fort Mountain State Park. The directions start from the dam.

TRAIL CONFIGURATION
Loop

SURFACE
Single track • 1.2 miles

HIGHLIGHTS
Rooty section, lake views, small bridge, varied users

TOTAL DISTANCE
1.2 miles

TIME ALLOWANCE
Beginner • 30 minutes
Intermediate • 20 mins
Advanced • 15 minutes

$2 PARK ENTRANCE FEE AND $2 BIKE USE FEE

★ =Start

Fort Mountain State Park
★
Chatsworth   Ellijay
GA 52
US 411   GA 5/515

Lake

2000'
1000'

Gold Mine

***A**ll atop Fort Mountain and part of the State Park's trail system, this wide single track loop is a real rollercoaster ride, with sections that will give your shocks a workout. You'll encounter a good bit of down-hill before the rollers begin, and the climb back to the start is a real doozy.*

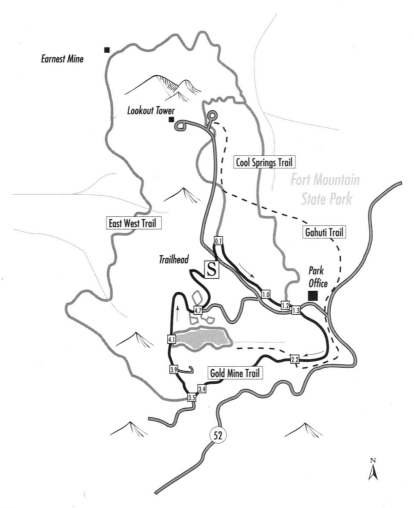

Earnest Mine

Lookout Tower

Cool Springs Trail

Fort Mountain State Park

East West Trail

Gahuti Trail

Trailhead

0.1

S

Park Office

1.0

1.2

1.3

4.7

4.1

2.2

3.9

Gold Mine Trail

3.4

3.5

52

N

START/FINISH
Fort Mountain State Park biker parking lot. The park is between Elijay and Chatsworth on GA 52.

TRAIL CONFIGURATION
Loop

SURFACE
Single track • 4.8 miles
Pavement • 0.7 miles

HIGHLIGHTS
Wide trail, rocky sections, climb at end, roller coaster hills, nice woods

TOTAL DISTANCE
5.5 miles

TIME ALLOWANCE
Beginner • 2+ hours
Intermediate • 1.5 hours
Advanced • 1 hour

$2 PARK ENTRANCE FEE AND $2 BIKE USE FEE

MILEPOSTS
- From start–ride across road and onto trail.
- Mile 0.1–bear right at fork.
- Mile 1.0–go straight at trails intersection.
- Mile 1.2–bear right as Cool Springs Trail enters.
- Mile 1.3–cross paved road.
- Mile 2.2–cross hiker only trail.
- Mile 3.4–trail enters from left. Continue straight.
- Mile 3.5–turn right on paved road.
- Mile 3.9–bear left at fork.
- Mile 4.1–cross dam.
- Mile 4.7–turn left on trail at entrance to camping.
- Mile 5.5–finish after switchbacky climb to trailhead.

★ =Start

Fort Mountain State Park
★
Chatsworth   Ellijay
GA 52
US 411   GA 5/515

Gold Mine Tr   cross dam

2000'
1000'

Cool Springs

You'll ride out to the edge of Fort Mountain for an amazing view before dropping straight off its face in a twisting, turning switchback descent that's sure to get your heart pounding. The trail then turns into a jumble of rocks that will test even the most competent of riders. The climb alongside a tumbling stream at the end should calm your nerves.

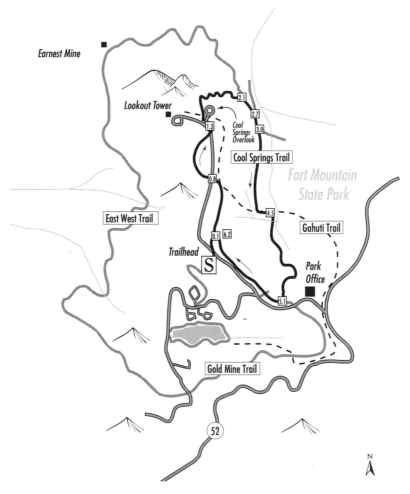

START/FINISH
Fort Mountain State Park biker parking lot. The park is between Elijay and Chatsworth on GA 52.

TRAIL CONFIGURATION
Loop

SURFACE
Single track • 6.3 miles

HIGHLIGHTS
Superb views, technical downhill, rock garden, waterfalls and cascades, tough climb

TOTAL DISTANCE
6.3 miles

TIME ALLOWANCE
Beginner • 3.5+ hours
Intermediate • 2 hours
Advanced • 1.5 hours

$2 PARK ENTRANCE FEE AND $2 BIKE USE FEE

MILEPOSTS
- From start–ride across road onto trail.
- Mile 0.1–bear left at trail fork.
- Mile 0.8–cross road.
- Mile 1.3–cross road at Cool Springs Overlook.
- Mile 2.1–bottom of switchbacks. Turn right.
- Mile 2.7–turn right on old road-bed.
- Mile 3.0–turn right on trail.
- Mile 4.5–turn right across creek.
- Mile 5.1–turn right on Gold Mine Trail.
- Mile 6.2–turn left to close loop.
- Mile 6.3–finish.

★ =Start

Fort Mountain State Park
★
Chatsworth   Ellijay
GA 52
US 411   GA 5/515

Cool Springs Overlook   Gold Mine Tr

2000'

1000'

East West

*Y*ou won't find many longer, steeper downhills than the one on this ride. After a good rolling ride through the woods, you'll drop right off the side of Fort Mountain down a powerline cut—hold on tight! Along the route are numerous abandoned talc mines.

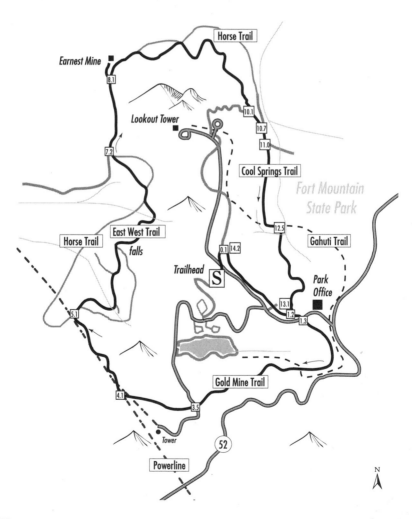

START/FINISH
Fort Mountain State Park biker parking lot. The park is between Elijay and Chatsworth on GA 52.

TRAIL CONFIGURATION
Loop

SURFACE
Single track • 11.4 miles
Forest road • 3 miles

HIGHLIGHTS
Superb views, long steep downhill, rock garden, waterfalls, old mines, tough climb

TOTAL DISTANCE
14.4 miles

TIME ALLOWANCE
Beginner • not advised
Intermediate • 3 hours
Advanced • 2.5 hours

$2 PARK ENTRANCE FEE AND $2 BIKE USE FEE

MILEPOSTS
- From start–ride across road and onto trail.
- Mile 0.1–bear right at fork.
- Mile 1.2–bear right as Cool Springs Trail enters.
- Mile 1.3–cross paved road.
- Mile 3.5–cross paved road.
- Mile 4.1–turn right along second powerline.
- Miles 5.1 to mile 7.2–bottom of hill. Turn right on roadbed. Go left. Go left again. Turn right. Bear left at falls. Horse trail crosses. Bear right.
- Mile 8.1–turn left to see Ernest Mine.
- Mile 10.1–Cool Springs Trail enters from right.
- Mile 10.7–turn right on old roadbed.
- Mile 11.0–turn right on trail.
- Mile 12.5–turn right across creek.
- Mile 13.1–turn right on Gold Mine Trail.
- Mile 14.2–turn left to close loop.
- Mile 14.4–finish.

★ =Start

Fort Mountain State Park
Chatsworth   Ellijay
GA 52
US 411   GA 5/515

Powerline Drop   Cool Springs Tr
2000'
1000'

GA 515 Corridor

Head north from Atlanta on I-575, which becomes GA 515, and you'll be driving up a corridor which has quite a few mountain bike trails within easy reach on either side of the highway. Hardly a route in this chapter is more than a ten-minute drive off a four-lane road. Don't get the impression that these are like urban trails. They're quite the opposite, leading into the backcountry and along the shores of several of north Georgia's lakes.

Farthest north is the town of Blue Ridge. Probably best known for the nearby lake of the same name, Blue Ridge is home to the Aska Mountain Bike Area, a large network of trails that snake over and around Rocky and Green Mountains and down to the shores

of Lake Blue Ridge. Expect to see plenty of riders at the trailheads at Aska. Also nearby—and technically in the Cohuttas—is the South Fork Trail. The fork it refers to is of the Jacks River, which flows through the Cohutta Wilderness. Because it's so close to Blue Ridge, I've listed it in this section.

South of Blue Ridge is Ellijay and apple country. This place has to have set some sort of record for the number of orchard houses selling apples in such a small geographic area. Each fall they celebrate with an apple festival.

The Cartecay River flows through the apple country, and along its banks in the Rich Mountain Wildlife Management Area (continues)

GA 515 Corridor

you'll find two of the oldest mountain bike trails in the state—the River Loop and the Red & White Loop. Cyclists have been riding these trails since the early 1990s. They were fun back then on the old clunkers, and they're still fun and challenging today. Over on the west side of Ellijay is Carters Lake and some of the newest mountain bike trails in the state. The trail at Ridgeway Recreation Area has been around awhile, but ground is still being broken for the one at Woodring Branch. Most of the work is being done by the Ellijay Chapter of SORBA, so you can be sure this trail will meet your expectations.

Closest to metro Atlanta and only a minute off the interstate is Blankets Creek. This trail too is a work in progress. You'll find a very nice intermediate loop, a beginner loop, and a soon to be completed advanced area. So close to Atlanta you're bound to run into plenty of cyclists, but as in most places, you see'll more folks at the trailhead than on the trail. Riders tend to spread out once in the woods.

South Fork
Green Mountain
Stanley Gap
Flat Creek
Long Branch
Hickey Knob
Red & White Loop
River Loop
Ridgeway
Woodring Branch
Blankets Creek
Blankets Creek Future

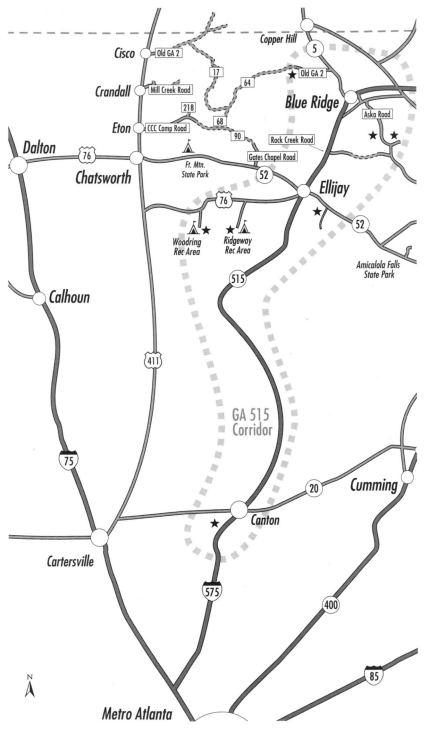

Cisco · Old GA 2

Copper Hill

5

17

64

Old GA 2

Crandall · Mill Creek Road

Blue Ridge

218

Aska Road

Eton · CCC Camp Road

68

90

Rock Creek Road

Dalton

76

Gates Chapel Road

Chatsworth

Ft. Mtn. State Park

52

76

Ellijay

52

Woodring Rec Area

Ridgeway Rec Area

Amicalola Falls State Park

Calhoun

515

411

GA 515 Corridor

75

20

Cumming

Canton

Cartersville

575

400

N

85

Metro Atlanta

*T*his is the only chance you get to ride alongside the Jacks River before it plunges into the Cohutta Wilderness. Wildlife openings make room for terrific views of the ridges above and you can plan on getting your feet wet at the stream crossings.

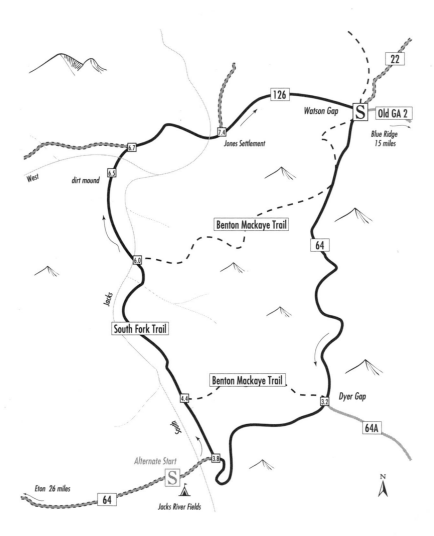

Mileposts

- From start–at Watson Gap, go south on FS 64.
- Mile 3.2–Dyer Gap. FS 64A exits to left. Stay on FS 64.
- Mile 3.8–at bottom of hill and just before crossing Jacks River, turn right onto South Fork Trail.
- Mile 4.4–Benton Mackaye Trail enters from right. It has a white diamond blaze.
- Mile 6.0–Benton Mackaye Trail exits to right. Continue on South Fork Trail.
- Mile 6.5–cross dirt mound onto woods road.
- Mile 6.7–ford river, ride up hill and turn right on FS 126.
- Mile 7.4–Jones Settlement. Continue straight on FS 126.
- Mile 8.1–finish.

START/FINISH

From Blue Ridge, take GA 5 north for 3.7 miles, turn left on Old GA 2 and continue another 10.5 miles to Watson Gap. *Alternate start: Jacks River Fields. There's better parking, but you have to drive another 4 miles on rough FS 64.*

TRAIL CONFIGURATION

Loop

SURFACE

Single track • 2.7 miles
Forest road • 5.4 miles

HIGHLIGHTS

Stream crossings, lush, boggy areas, small mountain community, nice views

TOTAL DISTANCE

8.1 miles

TIME ALLOWANCE

Beginner • 2 hours
Intermediate • 1.5 hours
Advanced • 1 hour

Green Mountain

*Y*ou start out with a choice of how to get to the top of Green Mountain. Left is hard; right is not so hard. From the top, it's a downhill rush to the shores of Lake Blue Ridge on terrific single track. You can turn around for an out-and-back to avoid a paved hill climb or continue on (as these directions suggest) for a loop.

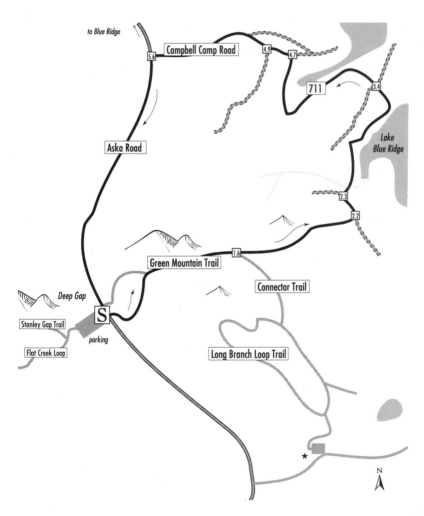

to Blue Ridge

Campbell Camp Road 5.6 4.9 4.7

711 3.4

Aska Road

Lake Blue Ridge

2.3

2.2

1.6

Green Mountain Trail

Connector Trail

Deep Gap

Stanley Gap Trail   S

parking

Flat Creek Loop

Long Branch Loop Trail

N

START/FINISH

From GA 515 in Blue Ridge, take Windy Ridge Road 0.1 miles south, turn left on E 1st Street, go 0.1 miles and turn right on Aska Road. It's 3.5 miles to the Deep Gap trailhead.

TRAIL CONFIGURATION
Loop

SURFACE
Single track • 3.4 miles
Forest road • 2.2 miles
Pavement • 1.9 miles

HIGHLIGHTS
Long downhill on single track, well marked, lake views, vacation homes, uphill to finish

TOTAL DISTANCE
7.5 miles

TIME ALLOWANCE
Beginner • 2 hours
Intermediate • 1.5 hours
Advanced • 1 hour

$2 USE FEE

Mileposts

• From start–cross Aska Road onto either one of the white-blazed Green Mountain Trails (the upper trail is hard and steep). They connect at the 1-mile point.
• Mile 1.6–connector trail to Long Branch exits right.
• Mile 2.2–old roadbed enters from right. Bear left.
• Mile 2.3–take a sharp right off old roadbed and cross small stream. Lake Blue Ridge will be to your right.
• Mile 3.4–Lower Green Mountain Trail trailhead. For loop ride, continue straight onto FS 711.
• Mile 4.7–turn left at T-intersection.
• Mile 4.9–turn right onto Campbell Camp Road.
• Mile 5.6–turn left onto Aska Road.
• Mile 7.5–finish.

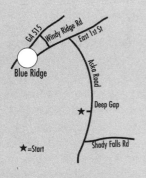

Stanley Gap

F*abulous single track makes this one heck of a trail! On this route, a paved downhill takes you to the Toccoa River before you go up, up, up on a forest road to the trail. You then ride over the top of the mountain and along the ridge on sweet single track.*

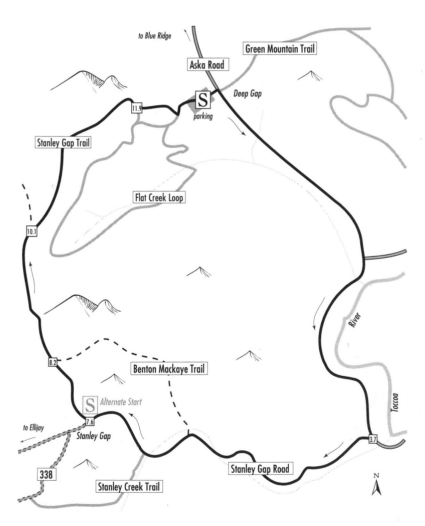

to Blue Ridge

Green Mountain Trail

Aska Road

Deep Gap

11.9

S
parking

Stanley Gap Trail

Flat Creek Loop

10.1

River

8.2

Benton Mackaye Trail

S Alternate Start

to Ellijay

7.6

Stanley Gap

Toccoa

3.7

338

Stanley Gap Road

Stanley Creek Trail

N

START/FINISH

From GA 515 in Blue Ridge, take Windy Ridge Road 0.1 miles south, turn left on E 1st Street, go 0.1 miles and turn right on Aska Road. It's 3.5 miles to the Deep Gap trailhead.

TRAIL CONFIGURATION

Loop

SURFACE

Single track • 4.9 miles
Forest road • 3.9 miles
Pavement • 3.7 miles

HIGHLIGHTS

Views, long rocky downhill, river rapids, vacation homes, small stream crossings

TOTAL DISTANCE

12.5 miles

TIME ALLOWANCE

Beginner • 3 hours
Intermediate • 2.25 hrs
Advanced • 1.5 hours

$2 USE FEE

Mileposts

- From start–turn right from trailhead parking area, downhill on Aska Road.
- Mile 3.7–turn right onto Stanley Gap Road. It's marked by a sign for Rich Mountain WMA. (Toccoa River Outpost is on the left.)
- Mile 7.6–Stanley Gap and Stanley Gap trailhead. Turn right onto Stanley Gap Trail. (white blazes).
- Mile 8.2–Benton Mackaye Trail enters right.
- Mile 10.1–Benton Mackaye Trail exits left.
- Mile 11.9–Flat Creek Connector Trail continues straight ahead. Turn left to stay on Stanley Gap Trail.
- Mile 12.5–bear left at trail junction to finish.

Flat Creek

You'll gradually climb to the head of Flat Creek before turning back down through the cove. Expect small stream crossings, tunnels of rhododendron, and a slip-slide ride through baseball-sized rocks. It's a steep climb back to the start of the loop.

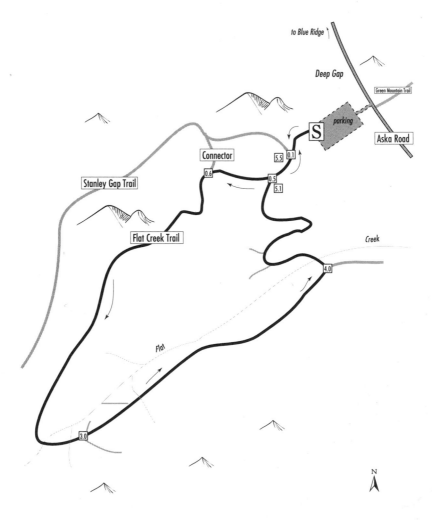

to Blue Ridge

Deep Gap

Green Mountain Trail

parking

S

Aska Road

Connector 5.5 0.1

0.6

Stanley Gap Trail 0.5

5.1

Flat Creek Trail

Creek

4.0

Flat

3.0

N

START/FINISH

From GA 515 in Blue Ridge, take Windy Ridge Road 0.1 miles south, turn left on E 1st Street, go 0.1 miles and turn right on Aska Road. It's 3.5 miles to the Deep Gap trailhead.

TRAIL CONFIGURATION
Loop

SURFACE
Single/double track • 5.6 miles

HIGHLIGHTS
Stream crossings, rhododendron tunnels, rocky section, steep but ridable uphill

TOTAL DISTANCE
5.6 miles

TIME ALLOWANCE
Beginner • 2 hours
Intermediate • 1.5 hours
Advanced • 1 hour

$2 USE FEE

Mileposts

- From start–ride out back of trailhead parking area.
- Mile 0.1–trail forks. Bear left onto Flat Creek Trail. It's marked with green and white dot blazes.
- Mile 0.5–bear right on double track to begin loop.
- Mile 0.6–Stanley Gap Connector Trail exits right. Stay on Flat Creek Trail.
- Mile 3.0–several abandoned woods roads enter and exit trail. Stay on Flat Creek Trail.
- Mile 4.0–turn left off double track onto single track, cross Flat Creek and bear left upstream.
- Mile 5.1–after steep climb, end loop and bear right.
- Mile 5.5–Stanley Gap Trail enters from left.
- Mile 5.6–finish.

GA 515 · Windy Ridge Rd · East 1st St · Aska Road · Blue Ridge · Deep Gap · Shady Falls Rd · ★=Start

cross Flat Cr

2000'

1000'

Long Branch

The first half of this loop follows an old skid road through a timber cut (read: hot and exposed on a sunny summer day, muddy when wet). After crossing the creek, you'll tunnel through shady rhododendron and hop over a few waterbars before a short climb back to the beginning of the loop.

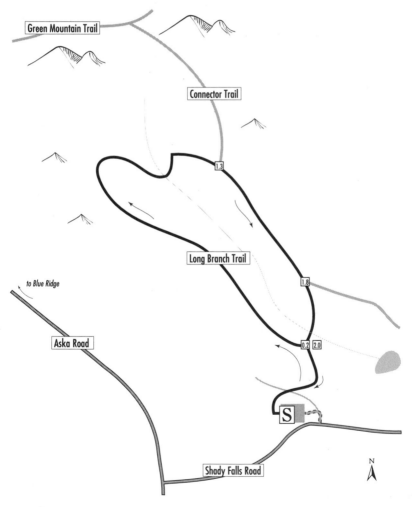

Green Mountain Trail

Connector Trail

1.3

Long Branch Trail

1.8

to Blue Ridge

Aska Road

0.2 2.0

S

Shady Falls Road

N

START/FINISH

From GA 515 in Blue Ridge turn south onto Windy Ridge Road. Go 0.1 miles, turn left on E. 1st Street, go 0.1 miles and turn right on Aska Road. Continue another 5.9 miles and turn left onto Shady Falls Road. Go 0.2 miles to the Forest Service parking area on the left.

TRAIL CONFIGURATION
Loop

SURFACE
Single track • 2.2 miles

HIGHLIGHTS
Views, stream crossing, waterbars, briar and mud potential, connects to Green Mountain Trail

TIME ALLOWANCE
Beginner • 45 minutes
Intermediate • 30 mins
Advanced • 20 minutes

$2 USE FEE

Mileposts

- From start–ride out of back of trailhead parking.
- Mile 0.2–fork. Start loop by taking trail to the left. The trail is marked with sporadic white and green dot blazes.
- Mile 1.3–Green Mountain Trail Connector enters from the left (marked by a green dot).
- Mile 1.8–bear right at trail fork.
- Mile 2.0–end loop. Continue back to trailhead.
- Mile 2.2–finish.

Connector Trail exits

2000'

1000'

Hickey Knob

*O*ne of the least known rides in the Aska area, this route is mostly forest road with just a bit of pavement. You'll ride over Hickey Knob and then down its other, waterbar-studded side. Around the base you'll pass through pretty fields, a pond, and an old homesite. These ruins constrast sharply with the modern lake homes you'll also pass en route to the finish.

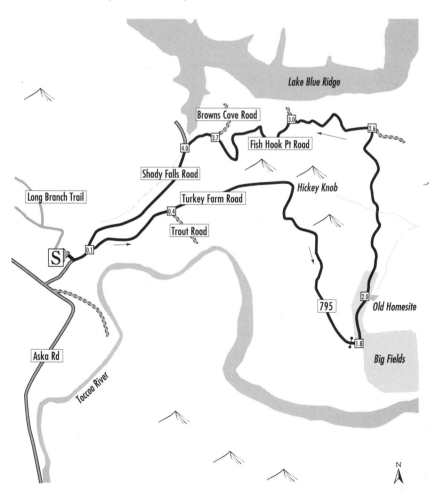

START/FINISH

From GA 515 in Blue Ridge turn south onto Windy Ridge Road. Go 0.1 miles, turn left on E 1st Street, go 0.1 miles and turn right on Aska Road. Continue another 5.9 miles and turn left onto Shady Falls Road. Go 0.2 miles to the Forest Service parking area on the left.

TRAIL CONFIGURATION
Loop

SURFACE
Forest road • 4 miles
Pavement • 0.6 miles

HIGHLIGHTS
4wd road, whoops, steady climb, old homesite

TIME ALLOWANCE
Beginner • 1 hour
Intermediate • 45 mins
Advanced • 30 minutes

$2 PARKING FEE

Mileposts

- From start–ride out of parking lot and onto Shady Falls Road.
- Mile 0.1–turn right on Turkey Farm Road. It's the first right turn and just beyond the powerline crossing.
- Mile 0.4–bear left. Trout Lane exits right.
- Mile 1.8–pass by gate and then bear left at big field. You'll keep the biggest part of the field to your right while you pass through the middle of a smaller extension.
- Mile 2.0–pass by pond and homesite. You'll see the ruins off to your right.
- Mile 2.6–turn left on Fish Hook Point Road.
- Mile 3.0–turn left to remain on Fish Hook Point Road.
- Mile 3.7–turn left on Browns Cove Road. It's paved here, but quickly becomes dirt again.
- Mile 4–turn left on Shady Falls Rd.
- Mile 4.6–finish.

Blue Ridge

GA 515 · Windy Ridge Rd · East 1st St · Aska Road · Deep Gap · Shady Falls Rd

★ =Start

Hickey Knob

Old Homesite

2000'

1000'

Red & White Loop

This short little loop is a great place for beginners to test their skills. You'll find sections of tight single track, but mostly the going is pretty easy. This route can be combined with the more difficult River Loop for an all-out ride. It gets its name from the alternating red and white blazes on the trees.

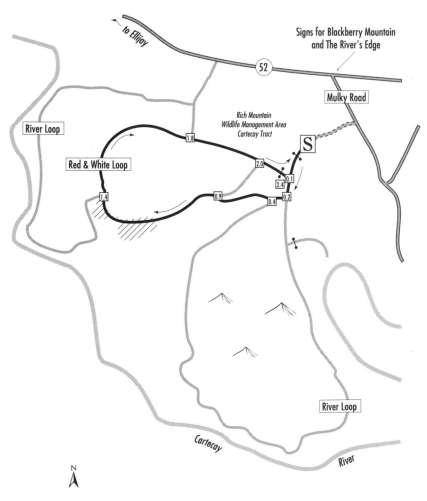

START/FINISH

From GA 515 in Ellijay, take GA 52 east for 3.2 miles and turn right onto Mulkey Road. Go 0.4 miles and turn right into the Rich Mountain WMA Cartecay Tract. Go 0.3 miles to start at the gate.

TRAIL CONFIGURATION

Loop

SURFACE

Single track • 2.2 miles
Gravel road • 0.4 miles

HIGHLIGHTS

Short technical stretch, grassy roadbed, wildlife openings, short hill climb

TOTAL DISTANCE

2.6 miles

TIME ALLOWANCE

Beginner • 45 minutes
Intermediate • 30 mins
Advanced • 20 minutes

Mileposts

- From start–ride past gate out gravel road.
- Mile 0.1–end of loop enters from right. Bear left.
- Mile 0.2–small clearing just past gate on right. Turn right onto red & white blazed trail.
- Mile 0.4–trail splits. Turn right. Look for blazes.
- Mile 0.9–little-used trail enters from right.
- Mile 1.4–wildlife opening. Trail to river exits left.
- Mile 1.8–trail to bike shop exits left.
- Mile 2.0–little-used trail exits back to right.
- Mile 2.4–gate; turn left.
- Mile 2.6–finish.

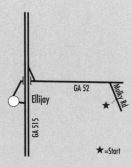

GA 52
Mulky Rd
Ellijay
GA 515
★=Start

River Loop exits

1000'

River Loop

his technical route alongside the Cartecay River packs a lot of punch. Take it easy on the hill down to the water's edge—it's very steep. And give yourself time to enjoy the river.

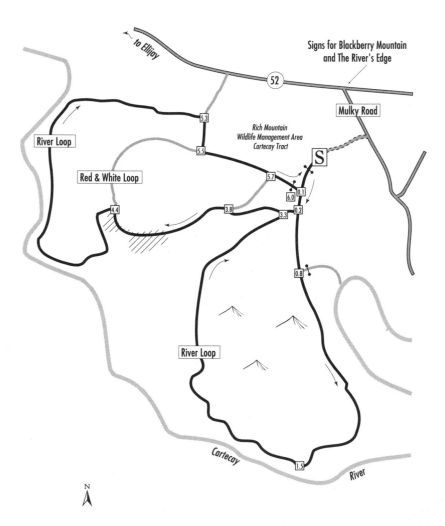

Mileposts

START/FINISH
From GA 515 in Ellijay, take GA 52 east for 3.2 miles and turn right onto Mulkey Road. Go 0.4 miles and turn right into the Rich Mountain WMA Cartecay Tract. Go 0.3 miles to start at the gate.

TRAIL CONFIGURATION
Loop

SURFACE
Single track • 5.6 miles
Forest road • 0.7 miles

HIGHLIGHTS
Great single track, one extremely steep downhill, Cartecay River, rapids, beaches, boggy areas, technical riding

TOTAL DISTANCE
6.3 miles

TIME ALLOWANCE
Beginner • 2 hours
Intermediate • 1.5 hours
Advanced • 1 hour

- From start–ride past gate out gravel road.
- Mile 0.1–Red & White Loop enters from right at the gate. Bear left.
- Mile 0.2–trail entering on right. Bearing left on the road.
- Mile 0.8–turnaround area with gated road entering on left. Continue across onto white blazed trail.
- Mile 1.5–steep downhill to river.
- Mile 3.3–turn left on Red & White Loop Trail.
- Mile 3.8–bear left on old road bed.
- Mile 4.4–just past double field, turn left.
- Mile 5.3–turn right. Left goes to bike shop.
- Mile 5.5–turn left on Red & White Loop.
- Mile 5.7–trail exits to right. Continue straight on.
- Mile 6.0–turn left at gate.
- Mile 6.3–finish.

Ellijay
GA 52
Mulky Rd
GA 515
★=Start

Cartecay River   Cartecay River

1000'

Ridgeway

*T*his fun, all-single-track loop follows the contours of the low ridges alongside Carters Lake. You'll find numerous short, steep ups and downs as well as plenty of twists and turns through the woods. There are many side trails, but the main trail is well marked and easy to follow.

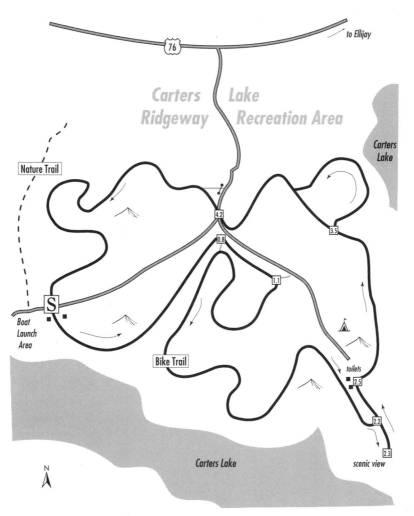

START/FINISH
Ridgeway Recreation Area boat ramp parking area on Carters Lake west of Ellijay, 8.5 miles off US 76.

TRAIL CONFIGURATION
Loop

SURFACE
Single track • 5.6 miles

HIGHLIGHTS
Views of lake, steep sections, easy to follow, very twisty

TOTAL DISTANCE
5.6 miles

TIME ALLOWANCE
Beginner • 2.5 hours
Intermediate • 1.5 hours
Advanced • 1 hour

$3 USE FEE

Mileposts

- From start–ride out between men's and women's outhouses following the orange posts. You'll follow the loop counterclockwise
- Mile 0.8–bear right just before road.
- Mile 1.1–trail from road enters from left. Bear right.
- Mile 2.2–turn right onto spur to scenic view.
- Mile 2.3–scenic view. Turn around and continue back past last milepost onto loop.
- Mile 2.5–at toilets, make hard right downhill.
- Mile 3.5–trail splits. You can go either way.
- Mile 4.2–cross road. A little farther up, a woods road will enter from the right.
- Mile 5.6–finish.

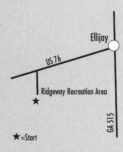

Ellijay

US 76

Ridgeway Recreation Area
★

GA 515

★ =Start

Scenic View

1000'

Woodring Branch

As this book went to press, this trail was in the early stages of development, with much of the work being done by the Ellijay Chapter of SORBA. Plans call for a good beginner trail with views of the lake and dam. Check the SORBA website at www.geocities.com/ellijaymba for the latest developments, or if you would like to volunteer to work towards its completion.

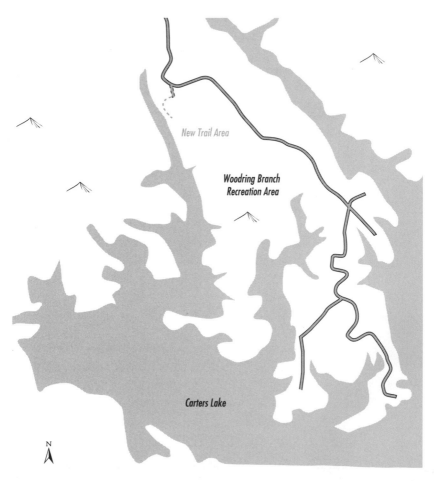

New Trail Area

Woodring Branch
Recreation Area

Carters Lake

N

START/FINISH
Woodring Branch Recreation Area on Carters Lake. Take US 76 west from Ellijay.

TRAIL CONFIGURATION
Loop

SURFACE
Single track

HIGHLIGHTS
Views of lake and many other highlights will certainly make this a nice trail.

TOTAL DISTANCE
3.5 to 5 miles

$3 USE FEE

Mileposts
• Not yet determined.

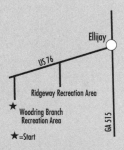

Ellijay

US 76

Ridgeway Recreation Area

★ Woodring Branch Recreation Area

GA 515

★ =Start

1000'

*T*his route is so twisty and curvy, you may not have time to look at the scenery. If and when you do look around, you'll see the pretty sight of Lake Allatoona off one side of the trail or the other. So close to Atlanta, expect to see plenty of other cyclists on the trail. The area closes at dark and the riding direction changes each day, so check the board before starting out.

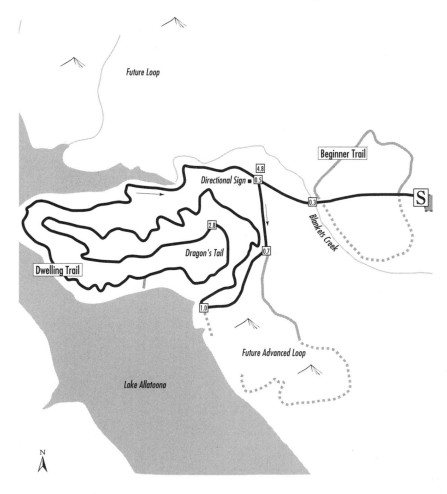

Mileposts

- From start–out past bulletin board and onto trail.
- Mile 0.3–cross Blankets Creek.
- Mile 0.5–directional sign board. These directions are given for a clockwise loop. Reverse them if it's a counter-clockwise day.
- Mile 0.7–the future Advanced Trail will exit left here.
- Mile 1.0–bear right. The lake is just ahead.
- Mile 2.8–enter the Dragons Tail. A particularly twisty section.
- Mile 4.8–close loop. Bear left to return to the trailhead.
- Mile 5.3–finish.

START/FINISH
Take exit 11 from I-575 west on Sixes Road. Go 1.8 miles to the trailhead parking on the left side of road.

TRAIL CONFIGURATION
Loop

SURFACE
Single track • 5.3 miles

HIGHLIGHTS
Views of lake, rutty sections, easy to follow, stream crossings, very twisty

TOTAL DISTANCE
5.3 miles

TIME ALLOWANCE
Beginner • 2 hours
Intermediate • 1 hour
Advanced • 40 minutes

$1 DONATION FEE

1000'

Blankets Creek Future

As this book went to press, half of the beginner loop at Blankets Creek was complete (as shown on the map below) and work on the advanced trail was just getting started. You can check at the trailhead or with SORBA (www.sorba.org) to find out about their current status. Better yet, volunteer to help finish them!

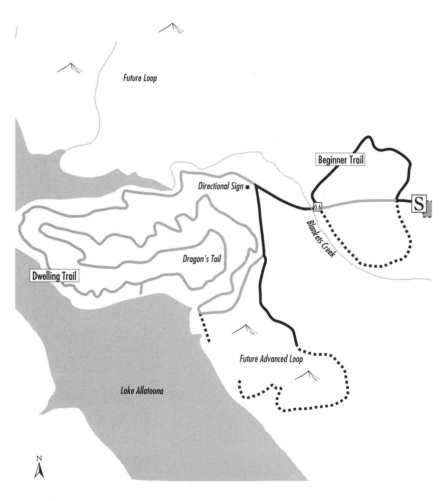

Future Loop

Beginner Trail

Directional Sign ■

0.6

Blankets Creek

S

Dragon's Tail

Dwelling Trail

Future Advanced Loop

Lake Allatoona

N

START/FINISH
Take exit 11 from I-575 west on Sixes Road. Go 1.8 miles to the trailhead parking on the left side of road.

TRAIL CONFIGURATION
Loop

SURFACE
Single track

HIGHLIGHTS
Views of lake, easy to follow, very twisty

TOTAL DISTANCE
1+ miles

TIME ALLOWANCE
Dependent on final trail length

$1 DONATION FEE

Mileposts

- From start–the Beginner Trail begins just past the trailhead bulletin board. Go about 100 yards and turn right.
- Mile 0.6–the trail splits just before joining the Dwelling Trail connector. You'll turn left to return to the trailhead. When the trail is completed, you'll continue straight across to follow Blankets Creek before looping back to the trailhead.

- The advanced trail follows Dwelling Trail (travelling counter-clockwise) for the first 0.7 miles. From there it will leave the trail on the left side and continue out to the shore of the lake, finally returning to rejoin Dwelling Trail at mile 1.

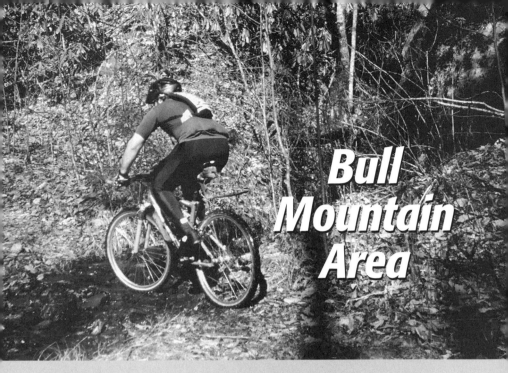

Bull Mountain Area

Nowhere in north Georgia is there a higher concentration of trails than in the Bull Mountain Area. This rugged mountainous region just north of Dahlonega forms the beginnings of the Appalachian chain. It is here that the more than 2100-mile footpath known as the Appalachian Trail has its southern terminus. Hikers begin their journey north at Springer Mountain just outside Amicalola Falls State Park and walk all the way to Maine. That's quite a feat for two feet. You'll see the bulk of the "through hikers" (those who plan to go the whole way in one season) heading out in March. Day and overnight hikers are seen any time of the year.

The region is also famous for gold. Our nation saw one of its first major gold rushes in 1928 after gold was discovered in north Georgia. By 1830 more than 300 ounces of pure gold were being produced per day. Unfortunately, the gold that was discovered here ultimately led to the removal of the Cherokee Indians to the West. Gold from nearby mines covers the courthouse dome in Dahlonega, and also the Capitol dome in Atlanta. Of course the rush is long over, but you can still find gold in the region's streams. It can even be said that the roads here are paved with the precious metal. Sand from the streams is used to produce cement, concrete and asphalt, and small quantities inevitably end up in the roads.

Mountain bikers will find a
(continues)

Bull Mountain Area

gold mine here as well. From the Bull Mountain Trailhead parking lot you can access well over 50 miles of trails and backroads. Routes will lead you along the sides of Springer Mountain, Bull Mountain, Jake Mountain and many more. You can ride the high forest roads that lead from gap to gap, or hop from creek to creek in the valleys far below.

From Amicalola Falls State Park you can ride a series of trails and jeep roads that will test both your riding and your direction-finding skills. Farther away, near the little mountain community of Suches, is the Cooper Creek region. Here you won't find so much single track, but the jeep road riding is superb as you link together loops through remote areas and quiet mountain farmland.

Canada Creek
Wahsega
Turner Creek
Jones Creek
Moss Creek
Winding Stair
Bull Mountain
Short Bull
Black Branch
Jake Mountain
Bull/Jake Combo
Amicalola Falls
Cooper Creek
Duncan Ridge
Sosebee Cove

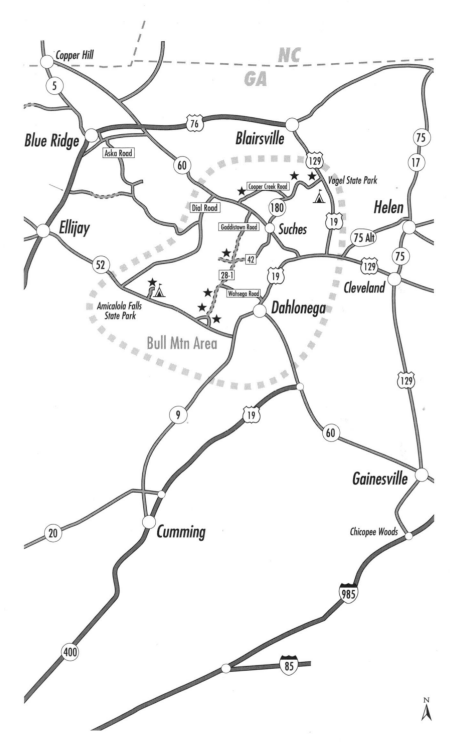

Copper Hill

NC
GA

5

76

Blairsville

75

Blue Ridge

Aska Road

60

129

17

Cooper Creek Road

Vogel State Park

Dial Road

180

Helen

Ellijay

Gaddistown Road

Suches

19

75 Alt

52

42

129

75

28-1

19

Cleveland

Wahsega Road

Amicalola Falls
State Park

Dahlonega

Bull Mtn Area

129

9

19

60

Gainesville

20

Cumming

Chicopee Woods

985

400

85

N

Canada Creek

It seems as if this ride is constantly going downhill (you pay later) while you work your way from where the Appalachian Trail crosses the high ridges. You'll find a hidden single track surprise as you traverse Canada Creek Road over to Pleasant Valley.

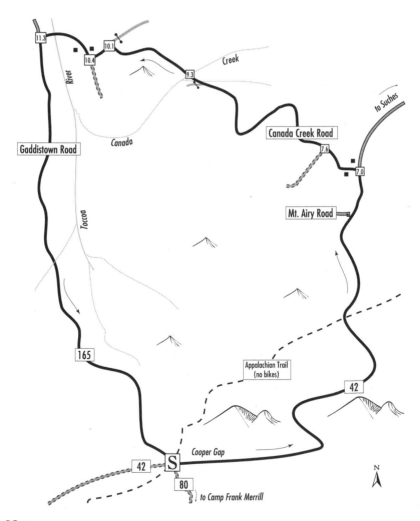

START/FINISH

From downtown Dahlonega, go 2.2 miles north on GA 60. Turn left on Wahsega Road. Go 8.5 miles and turn right onto FS 80 at Camp Frank Merrill. Go 2.8 miles to Cooper Gap.

TRAIL CONFIGURATION
Loop

SURFACE
Single track • 0.8 miles
Forest road • 11.4 miles
Pavement • 2.6 miles

HIGHLIGHTS
Great views, lots of downhill, old farm houses, stream crossing, streams, loose gravel

TOTAL DISTANCE
14.8 miles

TIME ALLOWANCE
Beginner • 3 hours
Intermediate • 2 hours
Advanced • 1.25 hours

Mileposts

- From start–ride east on FS 42 towards Suches. Do not ride on Appalachian Trail.
- Mile 7.0–turn left onto gravel Canada Creek Road. It looks like a driveway. Continue up past houses.
- Mile 7.6–road forks. Bear right.
- Mile 9.3–road closed barricade and an old, washed-out wooden bridge. Ford Canada Creek and go over dirt barricades up the grassy roadbed turned single track.
- Mile 10.1–cross over dirt barricade and bear left.
- Mile 10.4–road enters from left. Bear right past houses.
- Mile 11.3–turn left onto Gaddistown Road.
- Mile 14.8–finish.

Wahsega

*Y*ou may see some U.S. Army Rangers in training as you pass Camp Frank Merrill early in the ride. Be prepared to ford two streams, climb a couple of short but steep hills, and pass through a beautiful section of forest. This is also known as the Montgomery Creek ride.

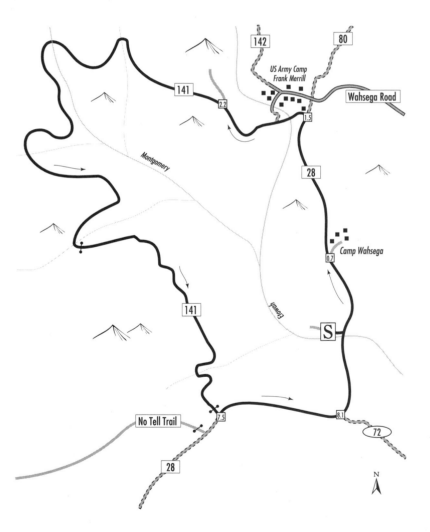

START/FINISH

From US Army Camp Frank Merrill take FS 28 south 1.7 miles to where the road crosses the Etowah River. There are parking and camp spots on the road upstream along the river.

TRAIL CONFIGURATION
Loop

SURFACE
Forest road • 8.5 miles

HIGHLIGHTS
US Army Ranger camp, stream crossings, short steep pitches, washouts

TOTAL DISTANCE
8.5 miles

TIME ALLOWANCE
Beginner • 2 hours
Intermediate • 1.5 hours
Advanced • 1 hour

Mileposts

- From start–ride north on FS 28 toward Camps Wahsega and Frank Merrill.
- Mile 0.7–pass 4-H Camp Wahsega.
- Mile 1.5–turn left at US Army Camp Frank Merrill gymnasium onto FS 141. Continue down across Etowah River and past landing field.
- Mile 2.2–road forks. Bear left downhill on FS 141.
- Mile 7.5–turn left onto FS 28.
- Mile 8.1–at road junction and mailboxes, bear left downhill on FS 28.
- Mile 8.5–finish.

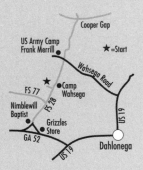

Camp Frank Merrill

cross Montgomery Cr

1000'

Turner Creek

*T*he abandoned woods roads of No Tell Trail loop you up and around and finally to the top of Turner Creek. Here the trail tightens up as it twists and turns down alongside and over the small stream that gives it its name.

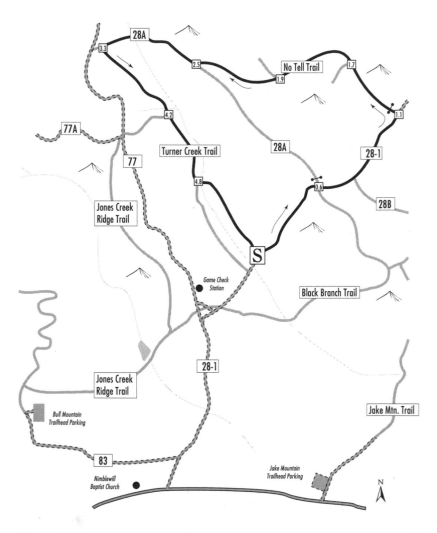

Mileposts

START/FINISH

From Nimblewill Baptist Church off GA 52 near Dahlonega, go 2.9 miles on FS 28-1 and start at end of Turner Creek Trail. *For a longer ride you may prefer to start at either the Bull Mountain or Jake Mountain trailhead parking area.*

TRAIL CONFIGURATION
Loop

SURFACE
Single track • 2.9 miles
Forest road • 2.4 miles

HIGHLIGHTS
Horse use, steep section, wooden bridges, tight single track

TOTAL DISTANCE
5.3 miles

TIME ALLOWANCE
Beginner • 1.5 hours
Intermediate • 1 hour
Advanced • 45 minutes

- From start–ride north on FS 28-1.
- Mile 0.6–FS 28A enters from left. Stay on FS 28-1.
- Mile 1.1–turn left around gate onto No Tell Trail.
- Mile 1.7–old woods road/trail enters from the left. Bear right.
- Mile 1.9–trail forks. Bear left down the hill.
- Mile 2.5–turn right onto FS 28A.
- Mile 3.3–just before road junction with FS 77, turn left down Turner Creek Trail.
- Mile 4.2–connector trail exits right. Stay straight.
- Mile 4.8–trail forks. Horses-only to right. Bikes to left. Go left down across bridge.
- Mile 5.3–finish.

Bull Mountain Area **97**

Jones Creek

You'll begin by riding down and across the dam to a secluded pond before tackling the trail atop Jones Creek Ridge. Stay on the lookout for wildlife as you complete the circle along the base of Bull Mountain.

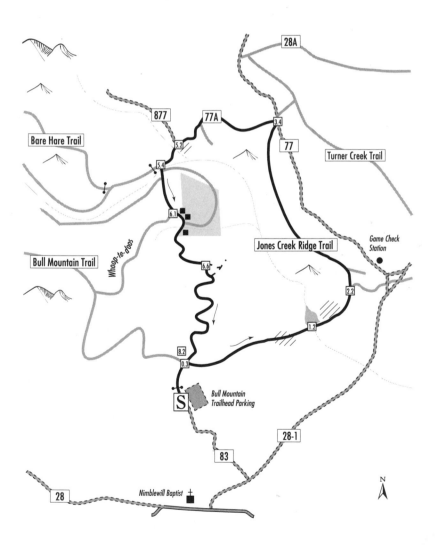

Mileposts

- From start–ride past gate and up FS 83.
- Mile 0.3–turn right past gate on Jones Creek Ridge Trail.
- Mile 1.2–cross dam and then go right around field.
- Mile 2.2–Moss Creek connector trail exits to right.
- Mile 3.4–turn left on FS 77A.
- Mile 5.2–at camping site, FS 877 exits right.
- Mile 5.4–cross Jones Creek and bear right as first road exits to left, then bear left as second road exits to the right. Climb up tricky, rocky roadbed.
- Mile 6.1–uphill whoop-te-doo trail exits right. Continue straight on and stay just right of shacks.
- Mile 6.6–gate. Turn right up trail then right on road.
- Mile 8.2–close loop. Continue straight.
- Mile 8.5–finish.

START/FINISH
From Nimblewill Baptist Church off GA 52 near Dahlonega, go 0.4 miles on FS 28-1 and turn left up FS 83 to the trailhead parking lot.

TRAIL CONFIGURATION
Loop

SURFACE
Single track • 3.3 miles
Forest road • 5.2 miles

HIGHLIGHTS
Horse use, nice views, pond, wildlife, great single track, rocky technical section, stream crossing

TOTAL DISTANCE
8.5 miles

TIME ALLOWANCE
Beginner • 3 hours
Intermediate • 2 hours
Advanced • 1.5 hours

$2 USE FEE

US Army Camp Frank Merrill • ★=Start
Wahsega Road
FS 28-1
FS 77 • Camp Wahsega
Bull Mtn Parking ★ FS 83
Nimblewill Baptist • Jake Mtn Parking
GA 52 • Grizzles Store
US 19
US 19 Dahlonega

Jones Cr Ridge
cross dam
2000'
1000'

Moss Creek

*I*f you want a real mixed bag of riding while in the Bull Mountain area, this is the one. You'll find climbs, descents, tricky switchbacks, swooping fast downhills, forest roads, tight single track—the works!

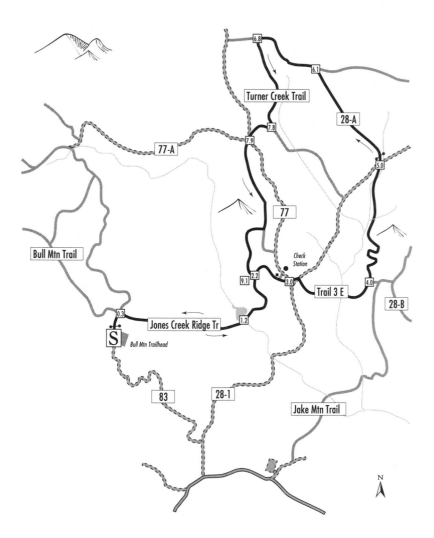

START/FINISH
From Nimblewill Baptist Church off GA 52 near Dahlonega, go 0.4 miles on FS 28-1 and turn left up FS 83 to the trailhead parking lot.

TRAIL CONFIGURATION
Loop

SURFACE
Single track • 7.1 miles
Forest road • 4.2 miles

HIGHLIGHTS
Horse use, nice views, pond, wildlife, great single track, ferny woods, small stream crossings

TOTAL DISTANCE
11.3 miles

TIME ALLOWANCE
Beginner • 3 hours
Intermediate • 2 hours
Advanced • 1.5 hours

$2 USE FEE

Mileposts
- From start—ride past gate and up FS 83.
- Mile 0.3—turn right past gate on Jones Creek Ridge Trail.
- Mile 1.2—cross dam and then go right around field.
- Mile 2.2—turn right on Trail 3-E connector.
- Mile 3.0—cross FS 77, then FS 28-1, and go around T-gate.
- Mile 4.0—bear left at trails jct atop ridge on 3-E.
- Mile 5.0—cross FS 28-1 onto FS 28 A.
- Mile 6.1—No Tell Trail enters from right.
- Mile 6.8—turn left on Turner Creek Trail.
- Mile 7.8—turn right on connector trail to FS 77.
- Mile 7.9—cross FS 77 on Jones Creek Ridge Trail.
- Mile 9.1—close loop. Bear right and return past previous mileposts.
- Mile 11.3—finish.

Winding Stair

This is forest road ridge riding at its best. You'll cruise around the tops of some of Georgia's highest peaks for over seven miles and pass through nine gaps. From the last one, Winding Stair Gap, you'll make a four-mile plunge.

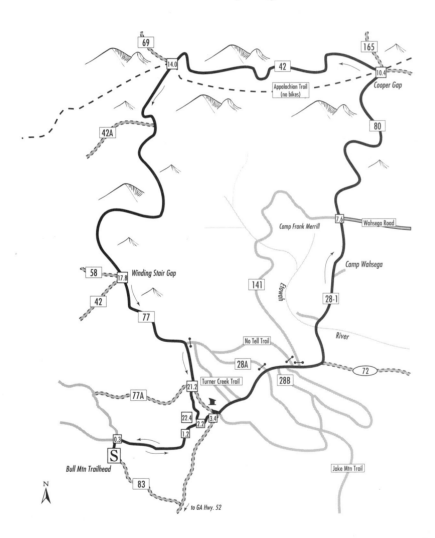

START/FINISH
From Nimblewill Baptist Church off GA 52 near Dahlonega, go 0.4 miles on FS 28-1 and turn left up FS 83 to the trailhead parking lot.

TRAIL CONFIGURATION
Loop

SURFACE
Single track • 6 miles
Forest road • 18.6 miles

HIGHLIGHTS
Ridge riding, views, rocky roadbed, long climb, long descent, Army Ranger camp, steep single track climb

TOTAL DISTANCE
24.6 miles

TIME ALLOWANCE
Beginner • 5 hours
Intermediate • 3.5 hours
Advanced • 2.5 hours

$2 USE FEE

Mileposts

- From start–ride past gate and up FS 83.
- Mile 0.3–turn right past gate on Jones Creek Ridge Trail.
- Mile 1.2–cross dam, then go right around field.
- Mile 2.2–Moss Creek connector trail exits to right.
- Mile 3.4–turn right on FS 77A, then left onto FS 28-1.
- Mile 7.6–pass US Army Camp Frank Merrill and continue across pavement onto FS 80.
- Mile 10.4–Cooper Gap. Turn left onto FS 42.
- Mile 14–FS 69 enters from right. Stay on FS 42.
- Mile 17.8–Winding Stair Gap. Big intersection of roads. Turn left, downhill onto FS 77.
- Mile 21.2–At FS 77A, turn right up Jones Creek Ridge Tr.
- Mile 22.4–close loop. Bear right and return past previous mileposts.
- Mile 24.6–finish.

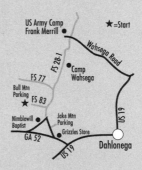

Bull Mountain

A three-mile, almost continuous climb; lots of single track; numerous small stream crossings; the sounds of waterfalls; miles of tight twisting downhill through the trees; rocky ascents; and beautiful scenery—this route has it all! It's easy to see why it's so popular.

START/FINISH
From Nimblewill Baptist Church off GA 52 near Dahlonega, go 0.4 miles on FS 28-1 and turn left up FS 83 to the trailhead parking lot.

TRAIL CONFIGURATION
Loop

SURFACE
Single track • 8.8 miles
Forest road • 2.7 miles

HIGHLIGHTS
Long hill climb, stream crossings, rhododendron tunnels, rocky sections, horse use, winter views

TOTAL DISTANCE
11.5 miles

TIME ALLOWANCE
Beginner • 3+ hours
Intermediate • 2.5 hours
Advanced • 1.75 hours

$2 USE FEE

Mileposts
- From start–ride around gate and up FS 83.
- Mile 0.3–turn left onto Bull Mountain Trail.
- Mile 1.6–whoop-te-doo trail enters from right.
- Mile 4.8–old trail enters up from the right. Bear left to begin Bull Mountain Extension (a.k.a.: Bare Hare Trail).
- Mile 8.8–pass gate and turn left onto FS 77A.
- Mile 9.0–pass gate, turn right across creek and continue straight up the hill on the rocky roadbed.
- Mile 9.3–whoop-te-doo trail exits right just before shack. Continue past shack, following the property line road between Forest Service and private land. Stay on the road. After passing the third shack on the left, the road leaves the property line and becomes a trail.
- Mile 9.9–turn right onto FS 83.
- Mile 11.2–pass entrance to Bull Mountain Trail.
- Mile 11.5–finish.

jct Bare Hare Tr

cross creek

2000'

1000'

◆◆◆

If you've always wanted to see where that tempting whoop-te-doos trail on the way up Bull Mountain leads to, here's your ride. Climb to the whoops, turn down them and have a blast. Keep low to the ground, watch your speed, and pay attention; someone may be on their way up.

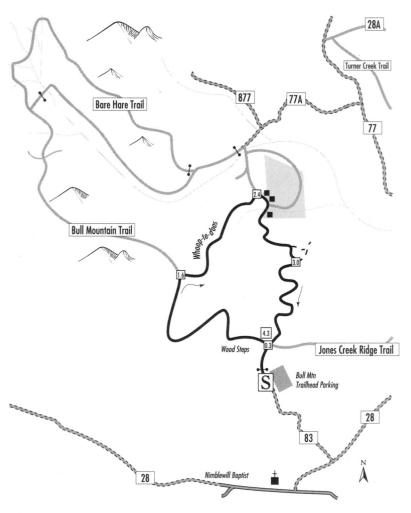

START/FINISH

From Nimblewill Baptist Church off GA 52 near Dahlonega, go 0.4 miles on FS 28-1 and turn left up FS 83 to the trailhead parking lot.

TRAIL CONFIGURATION
Loop

SURFACE
Single track • 4.6 miles

HIGHLIGHTS
Long hill climb, rhododendron tunnels, rocky sections, horse use, big whoops

TOTAL DISTANCE
4.6 miles

TIME ALLOWANCE
Beginner • 1.5 hours
Intermediate • 1 hour
Advanced • 45 min

$2 USE FEE

Mileposts

- From start–ride around gate and up FS 83.
- Mile 0.3–turn left onto Bull Mountain Trail.
- Mile 1.6–turn right down whoop-te-doo trail.
- Mile 2.4–turn right and continue past shack, following the property line road between Forest Service and private land. Stay on the road. After passing the third shack on the left, the road leaves the property line and becomes a trail.
- Mile 3.0–turn right onto FS 83.
- Mile 4.3–pass entrance to Bull Mountain Trail.
- Mile 4.6–finish.

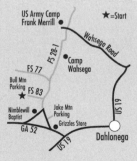

whoop-te-doos

2000'

1000'

Black Branch

Taking advantage of a formerly illegal trail, this beautiful route in the Bull/Jake Mountain trail system is a gem. You'll find a lot of rolling single track and lovely fern-filled woods as you roll down one side of Black Branch and back along the other.

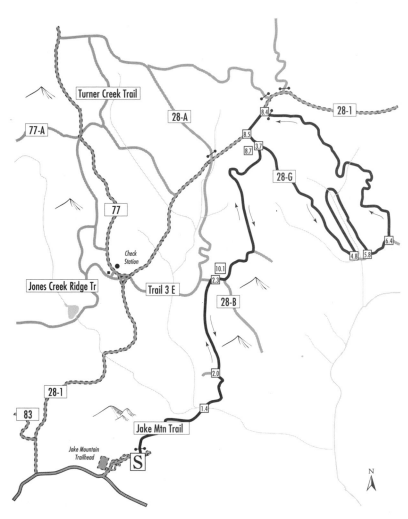

START/FINISH
Jake Mountain trailhead parking 1.8 miles from GA 52 on Nimblewill Church Rd, west of Dahlonega. *Alternate start: anywhere along FS 28-B.*

TRAIL CONFIGURATION
Lollipop

SURFACE
Single track • 8.9 miles
Forest road • 3.5 miles

HIGHLIGHTS
Horse use, steep downhill, big gravel section, great single track, ferny woods, stream crossings

TOTAL DISTANCE
12.4 miles

TIME ALLOWANCE
Beginner • 3 hours
Intermediate • 2 hours
Advanced • 1.5 hours

$2 USE FEE

Mileposts

- From start–ride past gate and up Jake Mtn. Trail.
- Mile 1.4–cross Jones Creek.
- Mile 2.0–trail exits left. Go straight along ridge.
- Mile 2.3–turn right on trail and then left on FS 28-B.
- Mile 3.7–turn right on FS 28-G.
- Mile 4.8–at bottom of hill turn sharp left on trail.
- Mile 5.8–turn left on trail just after it crosses creek.
- Mile 6.4–bear left at top of climb.
- Mile 8.4–turn left on FS 28-1.
- Mile 8.5–turn left on FS 28-B.
- Mile 8.7–bear right at entrance to FS 28-G.
- Mile 10.1–turn right on trail, then left at jct and return to start along Jake Mountain Trail.
- Mile 12.4–finish.

FS 28-G

cross Jones Cr

cross Jones Cr

1000'

Jake Mountain

*T*he ride is the namesake of the trail complex adjacent to the popular Bull Mountain trail. It traverses Jake Mountain Ridge before crossing over and connecting to the Bull Mountain system. You'll ford several small streams and soak in some nice views of the surrounding hills.

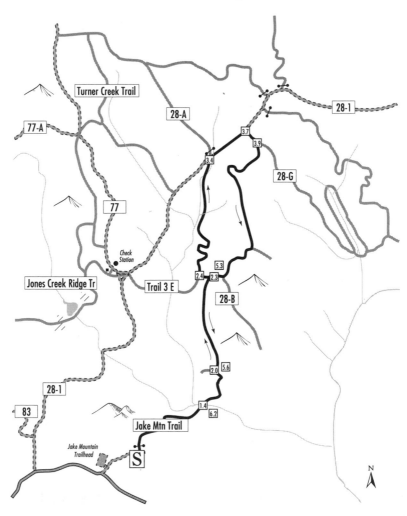

START/FINISH
Jake Mountain trailhead parking 1.8 miles from GA 52 on Nimblewill Church Rd, west of Dahlonega. *Alternate start: anywhere along FS 28-B.*

TRAIL CONFIGURATION
Lollipop

SURFACE
Single track • 5.7 miles
Forest road • 1.9 miles

HIGHLIGHTS
Horse use, switchbacks, great single track, ferny woods, stream crossings, old woods roads

TOTAL DISTANCE
7.6 miles

TIME ALLOWANCE
Beginner • 2 hours
Intermediate • 1.5 hours
Advanced • 1 hour

$2 USE FEE

Mileposts
- From start–ride past gate and up Jake Mtn. Trail.
- Mile 1.4–cross Jones Creek.
- Mile 2.0–trail exits left. Go straight along ridge.
- Mile 2.3–turn left on Trail 3-C.
- Mile 2.4–turn right Trail 3-E.
- Mile 3.4–turn right on FS 28-1.
- Mile 3.7–turn right on FS 28-B.
- Mile 3.9–FS 28-G exits left. Bear right.
- Mile 5.3–turn right on trail and then left at trails jct.
- Mile 5.6–trail exits right. Continue straight.
- Mile 6.2–cross Jones Creek.
- Mile 7.6–finish.

US Army Camp Frank Merrill • ★=Start
Wahsega Road
FS 28-1
• Camp Wahsega
FS 77
Bull Mtn Parking FS 83
Nimblewill Baptist • ★ Jake Mtn Parking
US 19
• Grizzles Store
GA 52
US 19 ○ Dahlonega

cross Jones Cr   cross Jones Cr
1000'

◆ ◆ ◆

Bull/Jake Combo

*T*his difficult but exhilarating ride encircles the entire Bull and Jake Mountain trail complex. You'll see a lot of everything and be plenty tired when you're done.

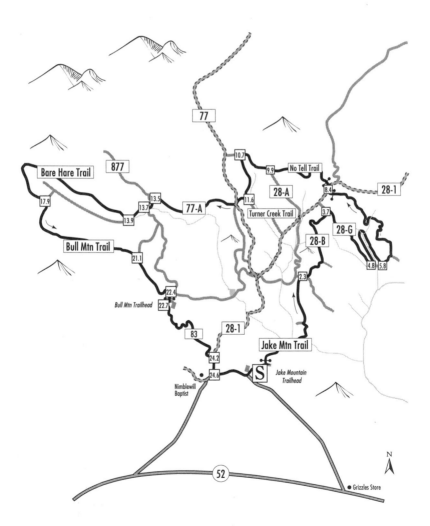

START/FINISH

Jake Mountain trailhead parking 1.8 miles from GA 52 on Nimblewill Church Rd, west of Dahlonega. *Alternate start: anywhere along FS 28-B.*

TRAIL CONFIGURATION

Loop

SURFACE

Single track • 17.6 miles
Forest road • 7.5 miles
Pavement • 0.5 miles

HIGHLIGHTS

Long hill climbs, stream crossings, whoop-te-doos, rocky sections, horse use, switchbacks, great single track

TOTAL DISTANCE

25.6 miles

TIME ALLOWANCE

Beginner • not advised
Intermediate • 5 hours
Advanced • 3.5 hours

$2 USE FEE

Mileposts

- From start–ride past gate and up Jake Mtn Trail.
- Mile 2.3–turn right on trail and then left on FS 28-B.
- Mile 3.7–turn right on FS 28-G.
- Mile 4.8–at bottom of hill turn sharp left on trail.
- Mile 5.8–turn left on trail just after it crosses creek.
- Mile 8.4–turn right on FS 28-1 then left around gate on No Tell Trail.
- Mile 9.9–turn right onto FS 28A.
- Mile 10.7–turn left down Turner Creek Trail.
- Mile 11.6–turn right up connector trail and ride across onto FS 77A.
- Mile 13.5–at camping site, FS 877 exits right.
- Mile 13.7–continue around gate up FS 77A.
- Mile 13.9–turn right past gate onto bottom of Bare Hare Trail.
- Mile 17.9–continue straight on Bull Mountain Trail.
- Mile 21.1–trail exits left. Continue straight.
- Mile 22.4–turn right on FS 83.
- Mile 22.7–Bull Mountain trailhead. Turn right past gate on FS 83.
- Mile 24.2–turn right on FS 28-1.
- Mile 24.6–turn left on paved road.
- Mile 25.6–finish.

2000'
cross Jones Cr
FS 77-A
Bare Hare Tr
1000'

Starting with a top-of-Georgia view, you'll do a little climbing, then a hidden ATV trail takes you into a beautiful valley. You're not there long before making an arduous climb up and over Frosty Mountain and back to your start at the falls.

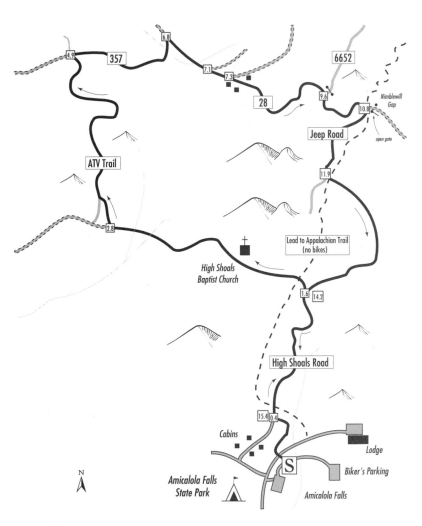

357

4.9

6.8

7.1

7.3

6652

28

9.6

Nimblewill Gap

10.8

Jeep Road

open gate

ATV Trail

11.9

2.8

Lead to Appalachian Trail (no bikes)

High Shoals Baptist Church

1.6   14.2

High Shoals Road

15.4   0.4

Cabins

Lodge

S

Biker's Parking

N

Amicalola Falls State Park

Amicalola Falls

START/FINISH
Top of falls bike parking lot at Amicalola Falls State Park.

TRAIL CONFIGURATION
Giant Lollipop

SURFACE
Single/double track • 6.2 miles
Forest road • 9.6 miles

HIGHLIGHTS
Waterfall view, stream crossings, ATV use, very rocky sections

TOTAL DISTANCE
15.8 miles

TIME ALLOWANCE
Beginner • 4.5 hours
Intermediate • 3 hours
Advanced • 2 hours

$3 PARK USE FEE

Mileposts

- From start–ride up bike trail from parking lot.
- Mile 0.4–turn right onto High Shoals Road.
- Mile 1.6–bear left at road fork to begin loop.
- Mile 2.8–ford two streams and then turn right onto ATV trail. It may not be marked with a sign.
- Mile 4.9–turn right onto FS 357.
- Mile 6.8–make 180° turn right onto FS 28.
- Mile 7.1–drive exits left. Bear right on FS 28.
- Mile 7.3–road forks. Bear right toward houses on FS 28.
- Mile 9.6–FS 6652 exits left. Stay on FS 28.
- Mile 10.8–Nimblewill Gap. Make 180-degree right turn onto jeep road and continue to climb. Do not go downhill. Do not ride on Appalachian Trail lead.
- Mile 11.9–road forks. Bear left.
- Mile 14.2–turn left onto High Shoals Road.
- Mile 15.4–turn left onto bike trail.
- Mile 15.8–finish.

Cooper Creek

*A*s you circle Cooper Creek Scenic Area, you may begin to wonder if there is a hill around every bend. Fortunately, none are too long and the wide forest road gives you plenty of room to maneuver.

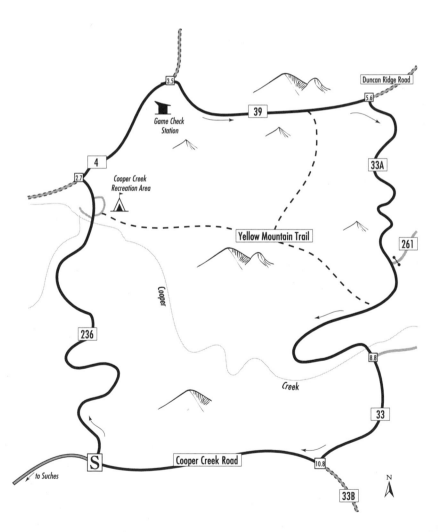

START/FINISH
Go 7.5 miles north of Suches on GA 60. Turn right onto Cooper Creek Road. Start at the junction of FS 236. Do not block the road.

TRAIL CONFIGURATION
Loop

SURFACE
Forest road • 10.8 miles
Pavement • 1.6 miles

HIGHLIGHTS
Recreation and scenic area, small cascades, views, rolling hills

TOTAL DISTANCE
12.4 miles

TIME ALLOWANCE
Beginner • 2 hours
Intermediate • 1.5 hours
Advanced • 1 hour

Mileposts

- From start–ride toward Cooper Creek Recreation Area on FS 236.
- Mile 2.7–just past Cooper Creek Recreation Area, turn right onto FS 4.
- Mile 3.5–after passing the game check station, take the first right, which is FS 39.
- Mile 5.6–turn right onto FS 33A.
- Mile 8.8–just after crossing Cooper Creek, you'll climb a hill. Partway up, bear right onto FS 33.
- Mile 10.8–pavement begins. FS 33B exits to the left.
- Mile 12.4–finish.

=Start

FS 236

Cooper Creek Road

GA 60

Suches

Cooper Cr Rec Area

cross Cooper Cr

2000'

1000'

Duncan Ridge

*S*tarting with a fast descent to Lake Winfield Scott, this ride goes down, down, down for close to ten miles before a steady climb up and onto Duncan Ridge. It's then a ridgeline ride on a rough road to the finish.

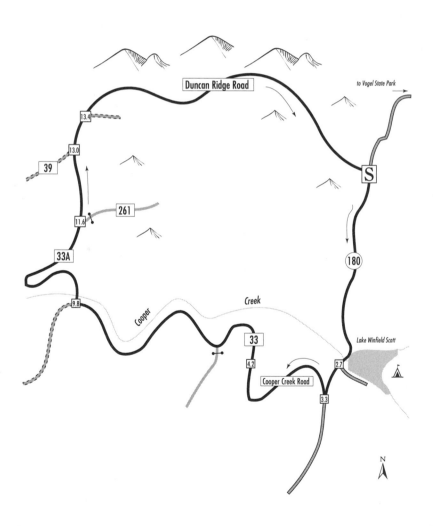

Duncan Ridge Road

to Vogel State Park

13.4

13.0

39

261

11.6

33A

S

180

9.8

Cooper

Creek

33

Lake Winfield Scott

4.2

2.7

Cooper Creek Road

3.3

N

START/FINISH
From Vogel State Park, go 3.5 miles on GA 180 to its jct. with Duncan Ridge Road. Start here.

TRAIL CONFIGURATION
Loop

SURFACE
Forest road • 16.3 miles
Pavement • 4.2 miles

HIGHLIGHTS
Long, fast, swooping downhill on pavement, rocky roads, views, ORV and 4WD use

TOTAL DISTANCE
20.5 miles

TIME ALLOWANCE
Beginner • 3 hours
Intermediate • 2.5 hours
Advanced • 1.75 hours

Mileposts

- From start–ride (downhill) on GA 180.
- Mile 2.7–Lake Winfield Scott on left.
- Mile 3.3–turn right onto Cooper Creek Road. 0.3 miles down the road will be a sign for Cooper Creek Wildlife Management Area.
- Mile 4.2–pavement ends and gravel FS 33 begins. Stay on this road for the next 5.6 miles.
- Mile 9.8–bear right onto FS 33A. Go downhill and cross Cooper Creek on a bridge.
- Mile 11.6–FS 261 exits right. Stay on FS 33A.
- Mile 13.0–junction Duncan Ridge Road (FS 39). Turn right.
- Mile 13.4–road exits right. Stay left on Duncan Ridge Road and continue to climb up the ridge.
- Mile 20.5–finish.

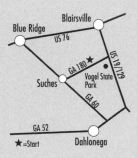

Sosebee Cove

A *steep descent on the highway brings you to the mouth of the cove. Soon, Slaughter Mountain looms ahead as you wind your way gradually back up, alongside Wolf Creek and through the length of the cove. The banked hairpin curves of GA 180 take you downhill back to your start at Vogel State Park.*

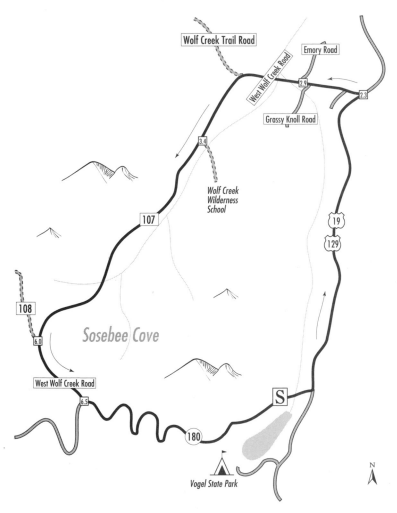

START/FINISH
You can start inside Vogel State Park (there's a parking fee) or at the pulloff 0.6 miles down GA 180 from the park.

TRAIL CONFIGURATION
Loop

SURFACE
Forest road • 3.6 miles
Pavement • 4.2 miles

HIGHLIGHTS
Highway, Vogel State Park, small cascades and waterfalls, one steep uphill, steep paved downhills

TOTAL DISTANCE
7.8 miles

TIME ALLOWANCE
Beginner • 2 hours
Intermediate • 1.25 hrs
Advanced • 45 minutes

Mileposts

- From start–ride back to US 19/129 and turn left down the hill. Use caution on the highway.
- Mile 2.3–turn left onto West Wolf Creek Road.
- Mile 2.9–Grassy Knoll Road enters left. Emory Road enters right. Continue straight over bridge onto forest road and then bear left at top of short hill. This is FS 107.
- Mile 3.4–road to Wolf Creek Wilderness School enters on left. Continue straight on FS 107.
- Mile 6.0–steep climb up to where FS 108 enters on the right. Stay on FS 107 by bearing to the left.
- Mile 6.5–turn left onto GA 180. It's all downhill from here.
- Mile 7.8–finish.

4

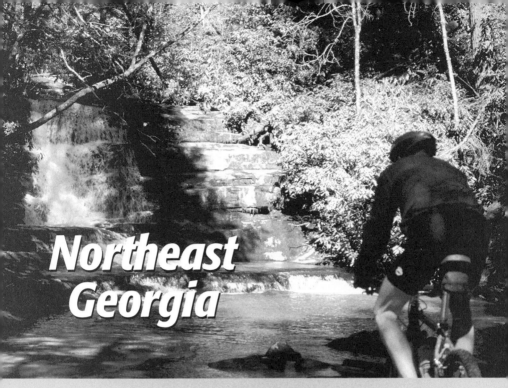

Northeast Georgia

Northeast Georgia offers everything from high mountain ridge riding, to trails alongside major whitewater rivers, to the nearest thing to urban trails in this guide. Diversity is the name of the game here.

Far to the northeast and along the Georgia-South Carolina border is the mighty Chattooga River. Here you can take a full day raft trip, or if you are a kayaker or canoeist, spend day after day testing your skills. Rapids rate in difficulty from 1 to 6 and this river has them all. If you head over this way to bike, you might also want to give thought to a river trip—you'll be glad you did.

Mountain bike trails and rides abound near the Chattooga and the town of Clayton. If you want to ride to the waterfall in the picture above, head for the Stonewall Falls Trail. Right next to it is a real roller coaster of a ride aptly named White Twister. Just down the road at the Tallulah Gorge you'll find three rides to choose from. Two are for more seasoned cyclists; one is the easiest ride in the book. It's on a paved rail-trail and is a great choice for families with young riders.

Head over the mountain to Helen and the riding changes again. Trails meander alongside the Chattahoochee River and up and over the Tennessee Divide (not to be confused with the Tennessee state line). Streams on one side of the divide flow to the Gulf of

(continues)

Northeast Georgia

Mexico, those on the other side flow to the Atlantic Ocean. If you're looking for one of the most difficult rides in this book, be sure to give the Hickory Nut ride a go. Also, be on the lookout for bears. This region has more than its share.

Finally, dropping down out of the larger mountains and into the foothills around Gainesville, you'll find an excellent network of trails (many folks just refer to the area as "Chicopee"). Chicopee Woods is an area within Gainesville that offers a lot to the community. There's the Elatchee Nature Center (one of the best in the state), an agricultural center, a golf course, and a finely-tuned trail system. Ride any trail here and you'll see where most the SORBA Gainesville Chapter's energy goes. The trails are very well built and maintained, and are an excellent example of good trail stewardship. In fact, these folks work on the trails so much that they've likely added a few miles since this book was printed.

Sandy Ford
Stonewall Falls
White Twister
Stoneplace
High Bluff
Shortline
Popcorn Creek
Wildcat Creek
Jasus Creek
Upper Hooch
Tennessee Divide
Helen
Ladyslipper
Devil's Backbone
Chicopee Woods
Zig Zag
Chicopee Ag Center
Gainesville College

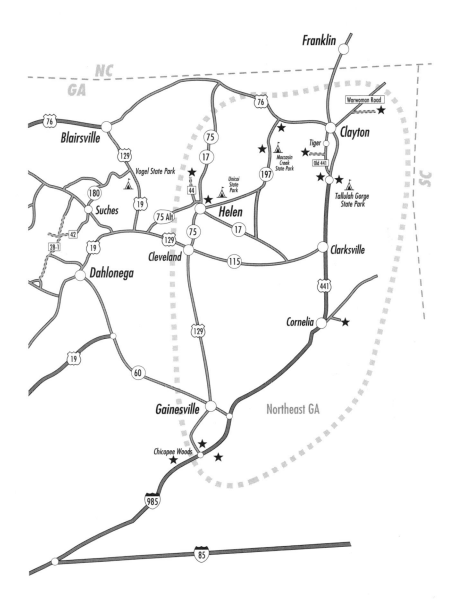

Sandy Ford is one of the few places you can access the Wild & Scenic Chattooga River by mountain bike. This backwoods route to the river is a lot of fun. You'll start with a bear of a climb, but the view and downhill that follow are worth it.

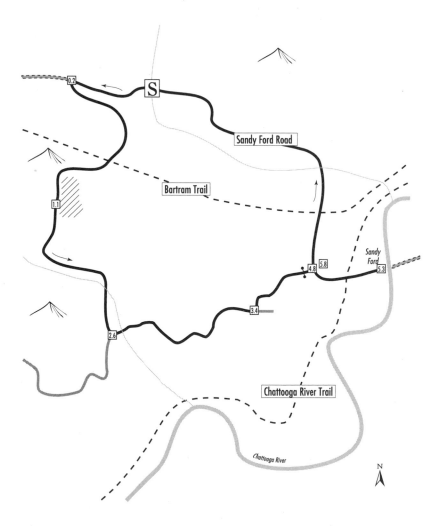

START/FINISH
Take Warwoman Road east out of Clayton 6 miles and turn right on Sandy Ford Road. Go 2.3 miles and start where road fords thecreek.

TRAIL CONFIGURATION
Loop

SURFACE
Double track • 2.4 miles
Forest road • 5.4 miles

HIGHLIGHTS
Short difficult climb, stream crossings, whoop-te-doos, big loose gravel sections, wild & scenic river

TOTAL DISTANCE
7.8 miles

TIME ALLOWANCE
Beginner • 3.5 hours
Intermediate • 2 hours
Advanced • 1 hour

Mileposts
- From start–ride back down Sandy Ford Road the way you came in.
- Mile 0.2–turn left on forest road.
- Mile 1.1–top of climb. Great view.
- Mile 2.6–bear left as trail enters from right.
- Mile 3.4–turn left on forest road.
- Mile 4.8–turn right on Sandy Ford Road.
- Mile 5.3–Sandy Ford of Chattooga River. Turn around here.
- Mile 5.8–pass forest road on left.
- Mile 7.8–finish.

★ =Start

2000'
1000'

Sandy Ford

Stonewall Falls

*E*verything about this ride is great except for the first mile, unless you like climbing up a loose gravel forest road. After the climb (and the view), the trail is pure bliss as you coast down through rhododendron tunnels and over whoops to the creek. There's even a steep technical descent thrown in. You'll finish beside a nice waterfall.

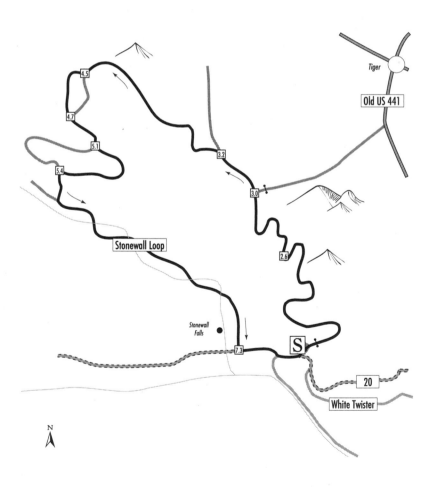

START/FINISH
From Tiger go 2.4 miles south on Old US 441 and turn right on FS 20. There's a pay station just down the road and a larger bike parking lot 1.3 miles farther on.

TRAIL CONFIGURATION
Loop

SURFACE
Single Track • 6.2 miles
Forest Road • 1.5 miles

HIGHLIGHTS
Big loose gravel, long climb, downhill whoop-te-doos, steep downhill, stream crossings

TOTAL DISTANCE
7.7 miles

TIME ALLOWANCE
Beginner • 2.5 hours
Intermediate • 1.5 hours
Advanced • 1 hour

$2 USE FEE

Mileposts
- From start–ride up past gate out of parking lot.
- Mile 2.6–top of climb and beautiful view.
- Mile 3.0–gated road enters from right. Bear left.
- Mile 3.2–bear left at fork.
- Mile 4.5–trail splits. Go right for easier climb.
- Mile 4.7–split trail reenters from the left.
- Mile 5.1–trail splits. Go left for technical descent.
- Mile 5.4–split trail reenters from right. Turn left.
- Mile 7.3–pass waterfall on right; turn left on FS 20.
- Mile 7.7–finish.

★ =Start

view

technical descent

2000'

1000'

White Twister

*I*magine a roller coaster for your bike—that's White Twister. A long series of swoops and turns, complete with a half mile climb, set you up for the plunge to Stonewall Creek. Just be sure not to get inverted. You finish up on an abandoned rail bed alongside tumbling Stonewall Creek with its numerous small falls.

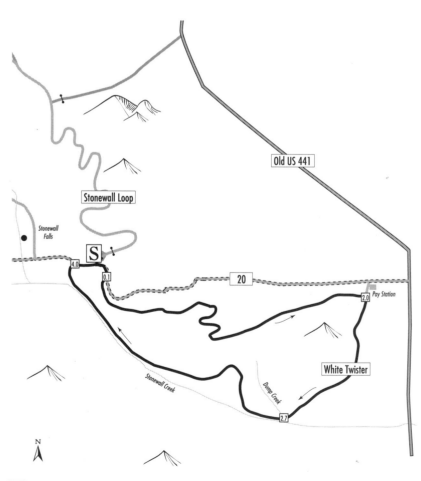

START/FINISH

From Tiger go 2.4 miles south on Old US 441 and turn right on FS 20. There's a pay station just down the road and a larger bike parking lot 1.3 miles further in.

TRAIL CONFIGURATION
Loop

SURFACE
Single Track • 4 miles
Forest Road • 0.3 miles

HIGHLIGHTS
tight turns, short hills, long downhill with whoops, creek and falls, galax-covered forest floor

TOTAL DISTANCE
4.3 miles

TIME ALLOWANCE
Beginner • 2 hours
Intermediate • 1.25 hrs
Advanced • 45 minutes

$2 USE FEE

Mileposts

- From start–ride back up the road you came in on.
- Mile 0.1–turn right on White Twister Trail (white blaze).
- Mile 2.0–turn right. A left takes you to the pay station. This is the top of the hill before the plunge.
- Mile 2.7–confluence of Dump Creek and Stonewall Creek. Cross Dump Creek on small wooden bridge.
- Mile 4.0–turn right on FS 20.
- Mile 4.3–finish.

★ =Start

Clayton
Tiger
FS 20
US 441
Old US 441
Wiley
Tallulah Falls

Pay Station

Creek Confluence

2000'
1000'

Stoneplace

*T*his is a great place to work on your skills. Starting at the huge and spectacular interpretive center, the trail follows along the top of the gorge before winding its way down to Lake Tugaloo and an old stone wall. Going down, you'll have momentum to help you through the rocky, rutty, technical sections. It's a long and gradual climb back to the top, so shift low and enjoy the scenery.

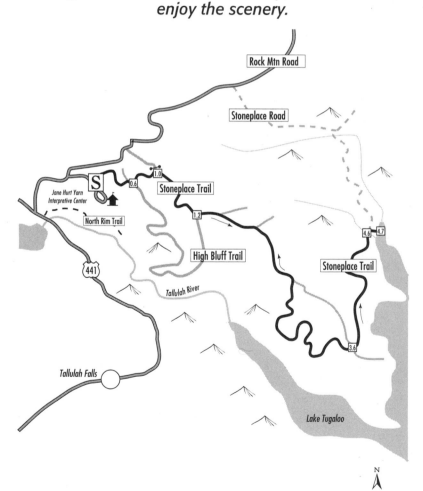

START/FINISH
Jane Hurt Yarn Interpretive Center off South Rock Mountain Road in Tallulah Gorge State Park.

TRAIL CONFIGURATION
Out and Back

SURFACE
Double track • 9.4 miles

HIGHLIGHTS
Washouts, loose rock, sandy areas, good views, Lake Tugaloo, long climb on return

TOTAL DISTANCE
9.4 miles

TIME ALLOWANCE
Beginner • 3 hours
Intermediate • 2 hours
Advanced • 1.25 hours

$4 USE FEE
You'll also need to pick up a biking permit in the information center.

Mileposts

- From start–ride out Stoneplace Trail and follow brown wooden post trail signs the entire way.
- Mile 0.6–High Bluff Trail exits to the right. Bear left.
- Mile 1.0–gate. Turn right on old road.
- Mile 1.2–High Bluff Trail exits to the right. Stay straight.
- Mile 3.6–4-way trail junction. Go straight.
- Mile 4.6–turn right down short but very steep and rocky hill to lake. A left leads into incredible blowdown.
- Mile 4.7–Lake Tugaloo and Stoneplace. Turn around here and return the way you came in.
- Mile 9.4–finish.

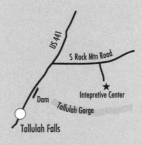

High Bluff

*T*his short ride never leaves the top of the gorge as it works its way out near the edge of the high bluffs. You'll get glimpses of the gorge through the trees, but most of the time you'll spend watching the trail.

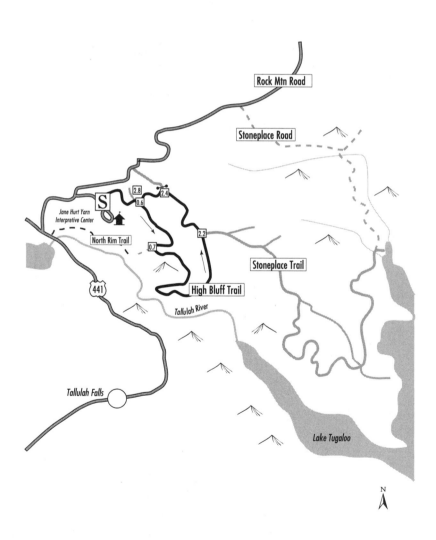

START/FINISH
Jane Hurt Yarn Interpretive Center off South Rock Mountain Road in Tallulah Gorge State Park.

TRAIL CONFIGURATION
Lollipop

SURFACE
Single/double track • 3.5 miles

HIGHLIGHTS
Washouts, loose rock, sandy areas, spotty views, small stream crossing

TOTAL DISTANCE
3.5 miles

TIME ALLOWANCE
Beginner • 1.25 hours
Intermediate • 45 min
Advanced • 30 minutes

$4 USE FEE
You'll also need to pick up a biking permit in the information center.

Mileposts

- From start—ride out Stoneplace Trail (yellow arrow blaze).
- Mile 0.6—turn right on High Bluff Trail (blue arrow blaze).
- Mile 0.7—turn sharply left on single track. The edge of the gorge is just ahead.
- Mile 2.2—turn left on Stoneplace Trail.
- Mile 2.4—you'll have passed through one gate. Here you turn left on the trail and pass beside a gate to your right.
- Mile 2.8—close up the loop and turn right to remain on Stoneplace Trail.
- Mile 3.5—finish.

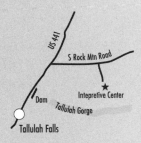

start High Bluff Tr
jct Stoneplace Tr
1000'

Shortline Rail-Trail

This is an excellent ride for beginning or young cyclists. It follows the old Shortline grade of the Tallulah Railway and—it's paved! Always in view are pretty river rapids or a quiet lake. You'll even get to cross a high suspension bridge over the river.

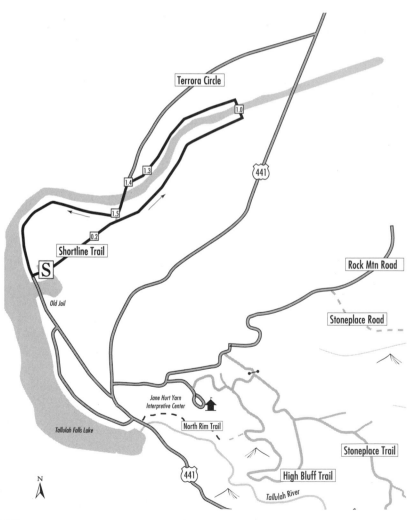

START/FINISH
Shortline Trailhead
Parking in day-use area
of Tallulah Gorge State
Park, off US 441.

TRAIL CONFIGURATION
Loop

SURFACE
Pavement • 2.4 miles

HIGHLIGHTS
Expect to see walkers,
parents pushing stroll-
ers and young cyclists,
cross suspension bridge,
read history of railroad

TOTAL DISTANCE
2.4 miles

TIME ALLOWANCE
Beginner • 45 minutes
Intermediate • 30 mins
Advanced • 15 minutes

$4 USE FEE

Mileposts

- From start–ride out Shortline Trail.
- Mile 0.2–pass under old iron bridge.
- Mile 1.0–cross Tallulah River on suspension bridge.
- Mile 1.3–pass upper trailhead.
- Mile 1.4–trail ends. Bear left on Terrora Circle.
- Mile 1.5–there's a little dirt path on the right that leads back to the rail-trail if you want to take it back to the start.
- Mile 2.4–finish.

Suspension Bridge

1000'

Popcorn Creek

***W**ith five major stream crossings, you're guaranteed to get your feet wet on this ride. The first four occur as you climb gradually along Dicks Creek. The last is at the end of a full five-mile descent. All are shallow and wide. You'll soak in some nice views as well.*

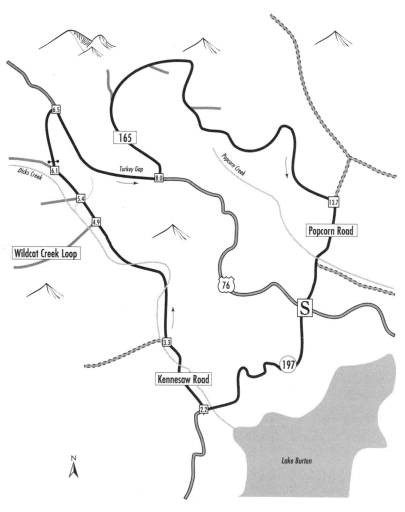

START/FINISH
At jct. of US 76 and GA 197, eleven miles west of Clayton.

TRAIL CONFIGURATION
Loop

SURFACE
Forest road • 11.4 miles
Pavement • 3.7 miles

HIGHLIGHTS
Long gradual climb, short steep pitch, stream crossings, very long downhill, views

TOTAL DISTANCE
15.1 miles

TIME ALLOWANCE
Beginner • 3.5 hours
Intermediate • 2 hours
Advanced • 1.5 hours

Mileposts
- From start–ride down GA 197.
- Mile 2.2–cross Dicks Creek and turn right on Kennesaw Lane. The land on either side is private, but the road is not.
- Mile 3.3–bear right at fork and enter WMA.
- Mile 4.9–bear right at fork. Wildcat Creek Loop enters left.
- Mile 5.4–bear right at fork in road.
- Mile 6.1–bear right at fork and go around gate.
- Mile 6.5–steep, gravelly climb. Turn right on US 76.
- Mile 8.0–turn left just past top of hill on FS 165.
- Mile 13.7–turn right on Popcorn Road.
- Mile 15.1–finish.

Wildcat Creek

*Y*ou'll begin this ride by climbing steadily for eight miles alongside the falls and cascades of Wildcat Creek. The most difficult part comes in the middle—a steep climb followed by a treacherous descent over loose rocks. Once along Dicks Creek it's an easy coast with a number of big shallow stream crossings to the finish.

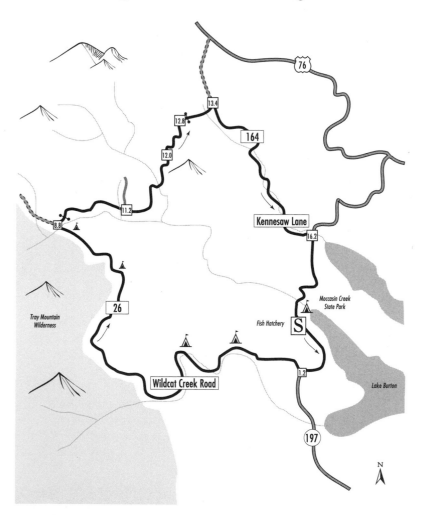

START/FINISH
Fish Hatchery next to
Moccasin Creek State
Park on GA 197 west of
Clayton.

TRAIL CONFIGURATION
Loop

SURFACE
Single/double
track • 4.6 miles
Forest road • 10.5 miles
Pavement • 2.7 miles

HIGHLIGHTS
Long strenuous climb,
very steep loose gravel
descent, highway, many
stream crossings

TOTAL DISTANCE
17.8 miles

TIME ALLOWANCE
Beginner • 6 hours
Intermediate • 3 hours
Advanced • 2 hours

Mileposts

- From start–ride south on GA 193.
- Mile 1.2–turn right on Wildcat Creek Road (FS 26).
- Mile 8.8–pass primitive campsite on right, cross small stream and turn right on a small road. There's a gate 100 yds ahead.
- Mile 11.2–woods road forks. Bear right.
- Mile 12.0–top of steep climb. Start steep downhill.
- Mile 12.8–continue past barricade.
- Mile 13.4–cross Dicks Creek and turn right on FS 164 (becomes Kennesaw Lane).
- Mile 16.2–turn right on GA 197.
- Mile 17.8–finish.

★=Start

US 76

GA 197

Clayton

Moccasin Creek
State Park
★ Fish Hatchery

US 441

border wilderness   steep climb

2000'

1000'

Jasus Creek

Bears! This area is heavily populated with them. The warning sign at the beginning of the ride can make you jump at the slightest sound as you travel around this gated double track loop.

START/FINISH
From Helen, drive 1 mile north on GA 17/75. Turn left onto Alt. 75. Cross river and turn right onto FS 44. Go 2.9 miles to Game Check Station on right.

TRAIL CONFIGURATION
Big Lollipop

SURFACE
Double track • 6.6 miles
Forest road • 5.4 miles

HIGHLIGHTS
Bear territory, gated-off roadway, wildlife openings, small cascades, cool streams, spotty views

TOTAL DISTANCE
12 miles

TIME ALLOWANCE
Beginner • 2.5 hours
Intermediate • 1.75 hrs
Advanced • 1.25 hours

Mileposts

- From start–ride north on FS 44.
- Mile 1.2–turn right and cross Low Gap Creek over bridge. Stay on FS 44. (FS 44A continues straight.)
- Mile 1.6–FS 44B enters on left. Continue on FS 44.
- Mile 3.7–turn left past gate onto FS 44B.
- Mile 10.3–a series of whoop-te-doos brings you back to FS 44. Turn right.
- Mile 10.7–cross Low Gap Creek and bear left.
- Mile 12.0–finish.

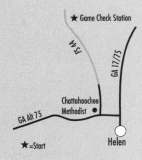

★ Game Check Station
FS 44
GA 17/75
Chattahoochee Methodist
GA Alt 75
Helen
★ =Start

FS 44B

Low Gap Creek

Low Gap Creek

2000'

1000'

Upper Hooch

*T*his route circles the upper reaches of the Chattahoochee River north of Helen. Be prepared to do some climbing on the far end of the loop. It's worth it; your legs will soon get a break while your brakes get a workout as you spin your way back down to the river.

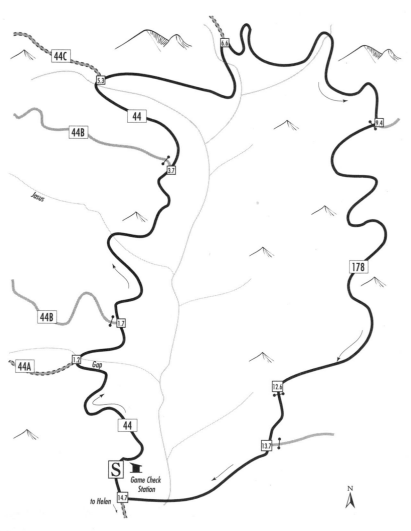

START/FINISH
From Helen, drive 1 mile north on GA 17/75. Turn left onto Alt. 75. Cross river and turn right onto FS 44. Go 2.9 miles to Game Check Station on right.

TRAIL CONFIGURATION
Loop

SURFACE
Forest road • 15.4 miles

HIGHLIGHTS
Chattahoochee River, small waterfalls, great views, timber cuts, wildlife openings

TOTAL DISTANCE
15.4 miles

TIME ALLOWANCE
Beginner • 3 hours
Intermediate • 2.25 hrs
Advanced • 1.5 hours

Mileposts

- From start–ride north on FS 44.
- Mile 1.2–bear right across Low Gap Creek.
- Mile 1.7–FS 44B enters from left. Stay on FS 44.
- Mile 3.7–the other end of FS 44B enters from left.
- Mile 5.3–FS 44C enters from left. Stay on FS 44.
- Mile 6.6–FS 44E enters from left. Stay on FS 44.
- Mile 9.4–turn right past gate onto FS 178.
- Mile 12.6–continue past gate.
- Mile 13.7–gated road enters from left. Bear right.
- Mile 14.7–cross river and turn right onto FS 44.
- Mile 15.4–finish.

★ Game Check Station
FS 44
GA 17/75
Chattahoochee Methodist
GA Alt 75
Helen
★=Start

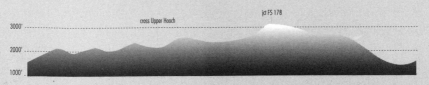

3000'
cross Upper Hooch
jct FS 178
2000'
1000'

Tennessee Divide

A long, steep climb takes you up to the Tennessee Divide. All the water behind you goes to the Gulf via the Chattahoochee River. All the water ahead of you goes to the Gulf via the Tennessee River. You'll cross and recross the divide before making a speedy return back down to the Hooch.

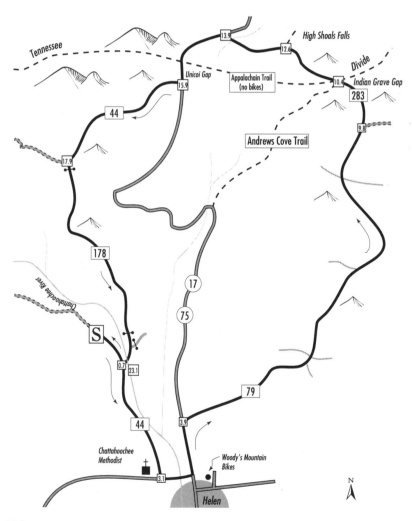

START/FINISH

From Helen, drive 1 mile north on GA 17/75. Turn left onto Alt. 75. Cross river and turn right onto FS 44. Go 2.9 miles to Game Check Station on right. *Alternate start: Woody's Mountain Bikes*

TRAIL CONFIGURATION

Loop

SURFACE

Forest road • 19.1 miles
Pavement • 4.7 miles

HIGHLIGHTS

Great views, long strenuous climb, loose gravel, highway, river and stream crossings, waterfall

TOTAL DISTANCE

23.8 miles

TIME ALLOWANCE

Beginner • 4 hours
Intermediate • 3 hours
Advanced • 2.25 hours

Mileposts

- From start–ride south, back down FS 44.
- Mile 0.7–start loop and continue on FS 44.
- Mile 3.1–turn left onto GA Alt. 75, then left on 17/75.
- Mile 3.9–turn right onto FS 79 and start 3-mile climb.
- Mile 9.8–road forks. Bear left downhill onto FS 283.
- Mile 10.4–Indian Grave Gap. Continue on FS 283. Do not ride on Appalachian Trail.
- Mile 12.6–side hike to High Shoals Falls.
- Mile 13.9–turn left onto GA 17/75. Start 2-mile climb.
- Mile 15.9–Unicoi Gap. Just past the gap, turn right on FS 44.
- Mile 17.9–turn left onto FS 178 and go around gate.
- Mile 23.1–turn right onto FS 44.
- Mile 23.8–finish.

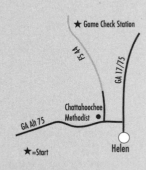

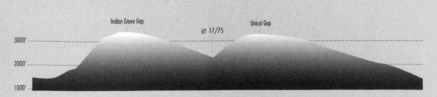

Hickory Nut

*T*his is one of the most difficult rides in north Georgia. A brutally long climb is followed by an equally brutal downhill with little relief. For much of the descent, hungry rocks are hiding in the trail just waiting for you to stop paying attention, then whammo!—you're down. If you like a challenge, you'll love it.

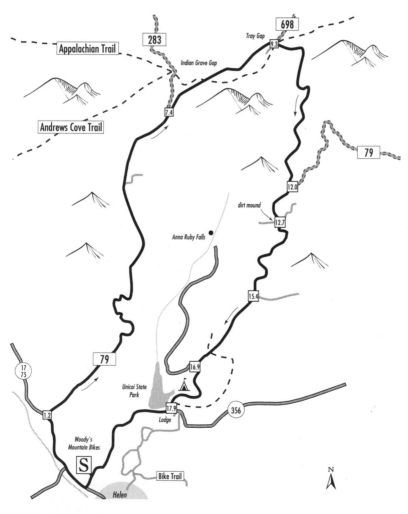

START/FINISH
Woody's Mountain Bikes, just off GA 356 between Helen and Unicoi State Park. You can get a shuttle from Woody if you want to skip the climb.

TRAIL CONFIGURATION
Loop

SURFACE
Single track • 4.2 miles
Forest road • 11.4 miles
Pavement • 3.9 miles

HIGHLIGHTS
Great views, long strenuous loose gravel climb, deadfalls, whoops, rocks, boulders, more rocks!

TOTAL DISTANCE
19.5 miles

TIME ALLOWANCE
Beginner • not advised
Intermediate • 4 hours
Advanced • 2.5 hours

Mileposts

- From start–go right on GA 356 then right on GA 17/75.
- Mile 1.2–turn right on FS 79 and start climbing.
- Mile 7.4–bear right to stay on FS 79.
- Mile 9.3–Tray Gap. End of climbing. Bear right to stay on FS 79. Don't go hard right on 4WD road or AT.
- Mile 12.0–turn right at T-intersection.
- Mile 12.7–road seems to dead end. A 4WD road goes left. There's a dirt mound to the right and a mound with a jumble of deadfalls straight ahead. Go straight by bearing left around the deadfalls and onto the trail.
- Mile 15.4–bear right at fork.
- Mile 16.9–turn left into state park on paved road.
- Mile 17.9–turn right on GA 356.
- Mile 19.5–finish.

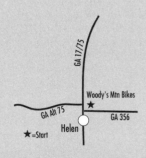

◆ ◆ ◆

Helen

*M*uch of this well marked trail has been used as part
of a big NORBA Nationals Race course. Don't let the
distance fool you; this is a tough ride. It's also a lot of
fun with its twists, turns, and stream crossings.

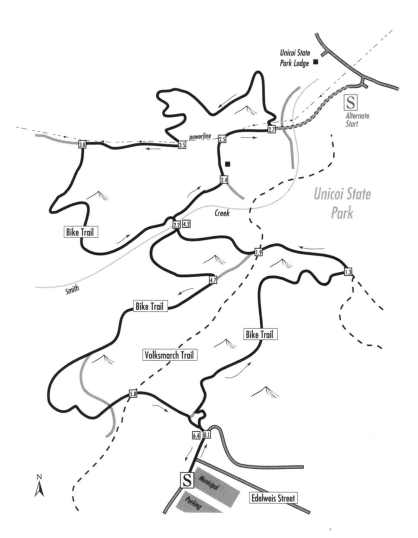

START/FINISH
Municipal parking lot on Chattahoochee Street, just past the visitor center in Helen.
Alternate start: Bike parking just below Unicoi State Park Lodge

TRAIL CONFIGURATION
Figure 8 Loop

SURFACE
Single track • 6.2 miles
Pavement • 0.3 mile

HIGHLIGHTS
Short steep hills, short pushes, many side trails, roots, washouts

TOTAL DISTANCE
6.5 miles (7.5 if you start in the state park)

TIME ALLOWANCE
Beginner • 2 hours
Intermediate • 1.5 hours
Advanced • 1 hour

$2 USE FEE
Payable at Unicoi State Park Lodge or the Helen Visitor Center

Mileposts

- From start–ride north, up Chattahoochee Street.
- Mile 0.1–just before hairpin turn, turn left onto bike trail and then take the right fork up the steep hill.
- Mile 1.3–turn left onto old woods road.
- Mile 1.9–cross Volksmarch Trail and then turn right down the side of the mountain.
- Mile 2.2–turn right, cross creek, then right again.
- Mile 2.4–turn left and ride up past old shack.
- Mile 2.5–turn right and then bear right at fork.
- Mile 2.7–turn sharply back uphill to the left.
- Mile 3.5–turn right on powerline.
- Mile 3.8–turn left up steep hill away from powerlines.
- Mile 4.2–turn right across creek and then bear right.
- Mile 4.7–turn right onto ridge.
- Mile 5.8–cross Volksmarch Trail.
- Mile 6.4–turn right on pavement.
- Mile 6.4–finish.

★ = Start

Municipal Parking

White St.

Chattahoochee St.

Munich St.

Main Street

Downtown Helen

cross creek

cross creek

2000'

1000'

Ladyslipper

*T*here are no tall mountains close by, but this route seems hilly just the same. You're either going up or down, and some of those ups, although short, are a grunt. In between, the smooth, pinestraw-covered trail is delightful and fast.

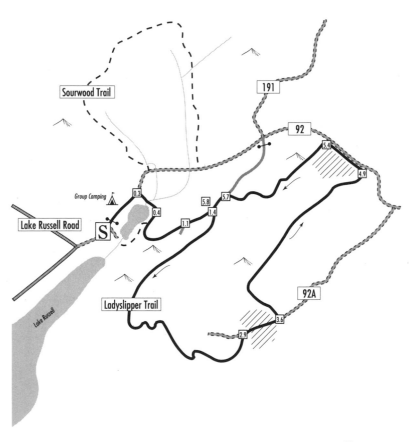

START/FINISH
Lake Russell Recreation Area trailhead parking, east of Cornelia off Dick's Hill Parkway.

TRAIL CONFIGURATION
Loop

SURFACE
Single track • 5.3 miles
Forest road • 1.1 miles
Pavement • 0.8 miles

HIGHLIGHTS
Horse use, washouts, steep climbs, whoop-te-doos

TOTAL DISTANCE
7.2 miles

TIME ALLOWANCE
Beginner • 3 hours
Intermediate • 2 hours
Advanced • 1.25 hours

$3 USE FEE

Mileposts

- From start–ride around gate and to group camp.
- Mile 0.3–turn right toward parking lot.
- Mile 0.4–ride out back of parking lot onto trail.
- Mile 1.1–bear left on old road bed.
- Mile 1.4–turn right on Lady Slipper Trail.
- Mile 2.9–turn right on FS 92A.
- Mile 3.6–turn on trail on far side of big timbercut.
- Mile 4.9–bear left just before FS 92 and parallel road.
- Mile 5.4–bear left up into the woods.
- Mile 5.7–turn left on roadbed.
- Mile 5.8–close loop. Stay on roadbed and follow previous mileposts to finish.
- Mile 7.2–finish.

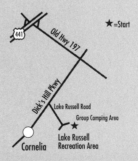

★ =Start

441

Old Hwy 197

Dick's Hill Pkwy

Lake Russell Road

Group Camping Area

★

Lake Russell
Recreation Area

Cornelia

parallel FS 92

1000'

Devil's Backbone

Formerly the Lake Trail, this route may be short but it still packs a bit of a punch. You'll ride out to the edge of the golf course (which took over the lake) and then back, paralleling the interstate. It's tight, twisty, and rooty most of the way.

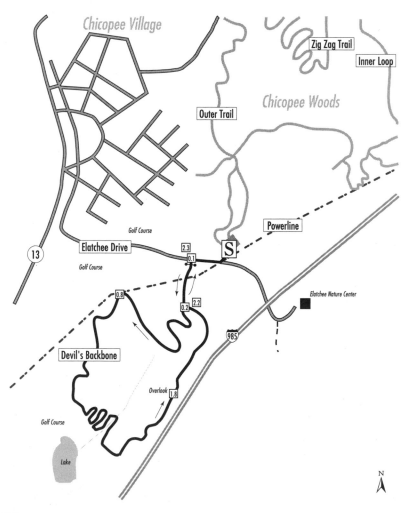

Chicopee Village

Zig Zag Trail

Inner Loop

Chicopee Woods

Outer Trail

Golf Course

Powerline

Elatchee Drive

13

Golf Course

2.3

0.1

S

Elatchee Nature Center

0.8

2.2

0.2

985

Devil's Backbone

Overlook 1.8

Golf Course

Lake

N

START/FINISH
Biker parking lot at Elatchee Nature Center on Elatchee Drive in Chicopee Village.

TRAIL CONFIGURATION
Loop

SURFACE
Single track • 2.2 miles
Pavement • 0.2 miles

HIGHLIGHTS
Roots, sharp turns, short steep hills, drainage crossings, interstate noise

TOTAL DISTANCE
2.4 miles

TIME ALLOWANCE
Beginner • 1 hour
Intermediate • 45 mins
Advanced • 30 minutes

$1 USE FEE
Chicopee trails are closed in wet weather. Check the biker hotline at 770-297-8319 before you leave home.

Mileposts

- From start–ride back down Elatchee Drive.
- Mile 0.1–turn left past gate onto old roadbed.
- Mile 0.2–cross powerline cut and turn right on trail.
- Mile 0.8–bear left just before powerline cut.
- Mile 1.8–interstate overlook.
- Mile 2.2–close loop. Continue straight across powerline cut.
- Mile 2.3–turn right on Elatchee Drive.
- Mile 2.4–finish.

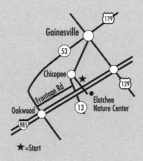

Overlook

1000'

Chicopee Woods

If you like pure single track, the Walnut Creek Outer Loop in Chicopee Woods is a fantastic ride. You hardly have time to notice much of anything, as your attention will be on the trail itself as it twists and swoops along.

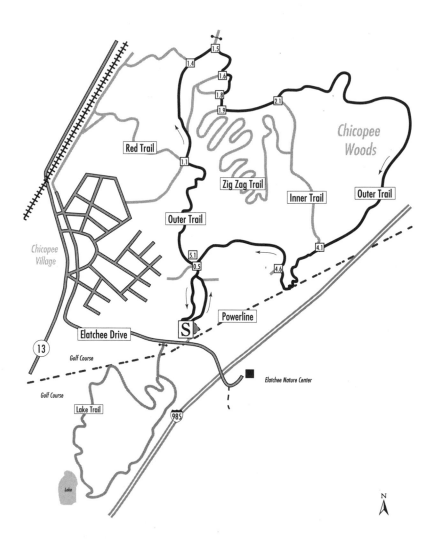

START/FINISH
Biker parking lot at
Elatchee Nature Center
on Elatchee Drive in
Chicopee Village.

TRAIL CONFIGURATION
Loop

SURFACE
Single/double
track • 5.6 miles

HIGHLIGHTS
Groomed trails, neat
bridges, no mud
(it's closed on wet
days), roots

TOTAL DISTANCE
5.6 miles

TIME ALLOWANCE
Beginner • 2.5 hours
Intermediate • 1.5 hours
Advanced • 1 hour

$1 USE FEE
Chicopee trails are
closed in wet weather.
Check the biker hotline
at 770-297-8319 before
you leave home.

Mileposts

- From start–ride out trail to right.
  Follow arrow.
- Mile 0.5–left on gravel road
  then right on trail.
- Mile 1.1–turn right on dirt road.
  Red Trail is straight across.
- Mile 1.4–road enters from left.
- Mile 1.5–turn right just before
  gate.
- Mile 1.6–turn left on blue blazed
  trail.
- Mile 1.8–bear left at fork following
  blue blaze.
- Mile 1.9–turn left at T-intersection.
  Zig Zag is right.
- Mile 2.1–turn left at T-intersection
  onto Outer Trail.
- Mile 4.1–bear left as Inner Trail
  enters from left.
- Mile 4.6–cross boardwalk bridges
  and turn right on road.
- Mile 5.1–close loop. Turn left
  toward trailhead.
- Mile 5.6–finish.

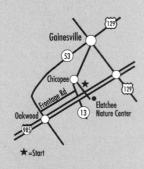

★=Start

Outer Tr   Old Dam
1000'

Zig Zag

As the name suggests, this is a very curvy trail and the most difficult of all the Chicopee Woods routes. As you zig and zag along you'll get to practice short bursts of speed with plenty of braking in between.

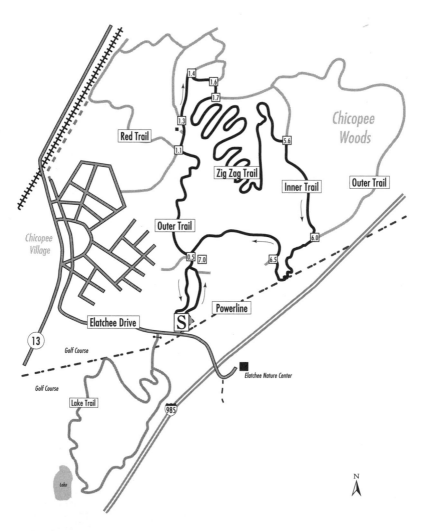

START/FINISH
Biker parking lot at Elatchee Nature Center on Elatchee Drive in Chicopee Village.

TRAIL CONFIGURATION
Loop

SURFACE
Single/double track • 7.5 miles

HIGHLIGHTS
Very twisty trail, rooty sections, groomed trail, neat bridges, dry days only!

TOTAL DISTANCE
7.5 miles

TIME ALLOWANCE
Beginner • 2.5 hours
Intermediate • 1.5 hours
Advanced • 1 hour

$1 USE FEE
Chicopee trails are closed in wet weather. Check the biker hotline at 770-297-8319 before you leave home.

Mileposts

- From start–ride out trail to right. Follow arrow.
- Mile 0.5–left on gravel road then right on trail.
- Mile 1.1–turn right on roadbed.
- Mile 1.3–shed left. Turn right off road bed on trail.
- Mile 1.4–turn right on trail.
- Mile 1.6–turn right on blue-blazed trail.
- Mile 1.7–turn right on Zig Zag Trail.
- Mile 5.6–turn right on Inner Trail.
- Mile 6.0–turn right to join Outer Trail.
- Mile 6.5–cross boardwalk bridges and turn right up gravel roadbed.
- Mile 7.0–turn left toward trailhead.
- Mile 7.5–finish.

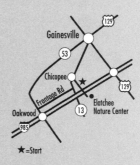

★=Start

Zig Zag Tr

Old Dam

1000'

*S*hort but sweet! This ride through the Ag Center woods offers one surprise after another—sudden drop-offs, log stacks, rock piles, and plenty of twisty turns. The white dirt of the trail shines in the piney woods. The trail is a work in progress; look for even more mileage in the future.

Chicopee Agricultural Center

Calvary Church Rd

Ag Center Trail

1.4

0.5

big hill climb

Lake

S

3.5

N

START/FINISH

From exit 20 on I-985 take Candler Rd to Calvary Church Rd. Go right 2.7 miles to the trailhead.

TRAIL CONFIGURATION

Loop

SURFACE

Singletrack • 3.7 miles

HIGHLIGHTS

Sudden dips, log stacks, rock piles, tight turns, laurel tunnels, one grunt of a climb

TOTAL DISTANCE

3.7 miles

TIME ALLOWANCE

Beginner • 1.5 hours
Intermediate • 45 mins
Advanced • 30 minutes

$1 USE FEE

Archery events close the trail 4-5 times a year. Check the biker hotline at 770-297-8319 before you leave home.

Mileposts

- From start–ride out from trailhead, past the information station and onto trail.
- Mile 0.5–cross woods road to remain on trail.
- Mile 1.4–cross woods road and then bear right to parallel road for a ways.
- Mile 3.5–enter clearing in woods.
- Mile 3.7–finish.

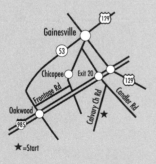

★ =Start

big hill climb

1000'

Gainesville College

*T*his may be the curviest three miles of single track in all of north Georgia as the trail takes maximum advantage of its allotted space. Following the outer edge of the college campus, it works its way down one side of Tumbling Creek and back up the other. A great introduction to single track riding.

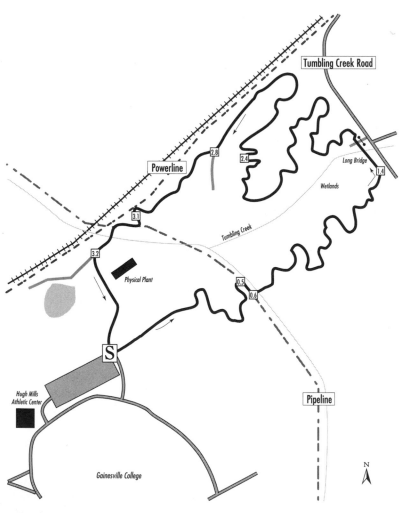

START/FINISH

Gainesville College. Park at the far end of the large lot past the athletic center and above the physical plant.

TRAIL CONFIGURATION

Loop

SURFACE

Single track • 3.5 miles

HIGHLIGHTS

Roots, sharp turns, wood bridges, short little hills, drainage crossings, wetlands and beaver activity, old home place

TOTAL DISTANCE

3.4 miles

TIME ALLOWANCE

Beginner • 1 hour
Intermediate • 45 mins
Advanced • 30 minutes

TRAIL CLOSED IN WET WEATHER

Mileposts

- From start–follow signs to bike trail and into woods.
- Mile 0.5–turn right where pipeline cuts through.
- Mile 0.6–turn left off cut and across bridge.
- Mile 1.4–cross wetlands on long wooden bridge.
- Mile 2.4–pass through old homesite.
- Mile 2.8–bear right as trail forks.
- Mile 3.1–swing through edge of powerline and then turn right into pipeline cut.
- Mile 3.2–leave woods and head up roadway.
- Mile 3.5–finish.

Gainesville
129
53
Chicopee
129
Gainesville College
★
13
985
Oakwood

★ =Start

Wetlands Bridge

1000'

Appendix

Local Bike Resources

NORTHWEST GEORGIA

• **Dalton Bicycle Works**
1107 E. Walnut Ave.
Dalton, GA 30721
706-279-2558
Close to Cohuttas, Pinhoti, and Pigeon Mountain

• **East Ridge Bicycles**
5910 Ringold Road
Chattanooga, TN 37412
423-894-9122
Close to Pigeon Mountain

• **Outdoor Pleasures**
117 South Wall St.
Calhoun, GA 30701
706-625-9907
Close to Pigeon Mountain

• **Bob's Bicycle Shop**
2203 Shorter Ave.
Rome, GA 30165
706-291-1501
Close to Pinhoti Trail

• **Pullen's Ordinary Bicycles**
105 Broad Street
Rome, GA 30161
706-234-2453
Close to Pinhoti Trail

THE COHUTTAS & GA 515 CORRIDOR

• **Cartecay Bicycle Shop**
4027 Hwy. 52 E
Ellijay, GA 30540
706-635-BIKE
888-276-2453
Close to Cohuttas, Carters Lake, Aska Trails, Amicalola Falls, and Bull Mountain Trails

• **Cycle South**
4295A Old Hwy. 76
Blue Ridge, GA 30513
706-632-3533
Close to Aska Trails, Cohuttas and Ellijay

BULL MOUNTAIN AREA

- **Mountain Adventures Cyclery**
  52 Clayton Drive
  Dahlonega, GA 30533
  706-864-8525
  Close to Amicalola Falls, Bull Mountain Trails and Helen

NORTHEAST GEORGIA

- **Bike Town USA**
  1604 Dawsonville Hwy.
  Gainesville, GA 30501
  770-532-7090
  Close to Chicopee Woods

- **Woody's Mountain Bikes**
  Highway 356
  Helen, GA 30545
  706-878-3715
  Close to Helen Trails

- **Cycle South**
  4295A Old Hwy. 76
  Blue Ridge, GA 30513
  706-632-3533
  Close to Aska Trails, Cohuttas and Ellijay

ADVOCACY GROUPS

- **SORBA**
  PO Box 1358
  Gainesville, GA 30503
  770-718-3674
  www.sorba.org

Lodging & Camping

When you're heading to a mountain bike destination, finding the perfect place to stay can be just about as important as finding the best trails. The towns and counties of north Georgia offer a huge range of accommodations—from rustic cabins and mountain lodges to campgrounds and primitive camping. You'll find the variety of eating establishments runs the gamut as well. Because I can't possibly guess just what type of place you are looking for, I've listed the addresses, phone numbers, and web addresses of the area chambers of commerce as well as the various state parks with mountain bike trails. When looking for up-to-date information on a place to stay or recommendations on places to eat, the local chamber is the best place to start. Give these folks a call and tell them what you're looking for. They can steer you in the right direction.

If you're camping at a primitive site or staying in a national forest campground on a weekend, it's a good idea to find your camping spot first and then go out for your ride. Just about everywhere else, it's possible to make reservations. You can bet that if the weather is fine, you're not the only one planning a trip to the mountains; lots of other folks will be looking for accommodations, too. Better to make the reservation ahead and avoid spending half your riding time looking for a place to stay.

CHAMBERS OF COMMERCE

NORTHWEST GEORGIA

- **LaFayette**
P.O. Box 430
Rock Spring, GA 30739
706-375-7702
www.walkercochamber.com

- **Dalton**
524 Holiday Ave.
Dalton, GA 30720
706-278-7373
www.nwgeorgia.com/
daltonwhitfieldchamber

- **Rome**
1 Riverside Pkwy.
Rome, GA 30161
706-291-7663

THE COHUTTAS & GA 515 CORRIDOR

- **Chatsworth**
126 North Third Ave.
Chatsworth, GA 30705
706-695-6060
www.mchamber@northga.net

- **Ellijay**
P.O. Box 505
Ellijay, GA 30540
706-635-7400
www.gilmerchamber.com

- **Blue Ridge**
P.O. Box 875
Blue Ridge, GA 30513
800-899-6867
www.blueridgemountains.com

BULL MOUNTAIN AREA

- **Dahlonega**
13 South Park St., Dept G
Dahlonega, GA 30533
706-864-3513
www.dahlonega.org

NORTHEAST GEORGIA

- **Helen**
P.O. Box 730
Helen, GA 30545
706-878-2521
www.HelenGeorgia.net

- **Clayton**
P.O. Box 761
Clayton, GA 30525
706-782-4812
www.gamountains.com/rabun

- **Gainesville**
P.O. Box 374
770-532-6206
www.ghcc.com

GEORGIA STATE PARKS

Georgia has an excellent system of state parks that feature not only recreational opportunities, but a wide range of overnight accommodations as well. Each park in north Georgia has primitive camping, full-hookup camping, and rental cottages. Of those, several have lodges, conference centers, and restaurants. It's wise to call ahead for reservations, especially for the summer or fall leaf seasons. Call 800-864-7275 for all parks or find them on the web at www.gastateparks.org.

• **Unicoi State Park & Lodge**
  P.O. Box 1029
  Helen, GA 30545
  706-878-2824
  www.ngeorgia.com/parks/
  unicoi.html

• **Vogel State Park**
  Route 1, Box 1230
  Blairsville, GA 30512
  706-745-2628
  www.ngeorgia.com/parks/
  vogel.html

• **Amicalola Falls State Park**
  Star Route, Box 215
  Dawsonville, GA 30534
  706-265-8888
  www.ngeorgia.com/parks/
  amicalola.html

• **Tallulah Gorge State Park**
  P.O. Box 248
  Tallulah Falls, GA 30573
  706-754-7970
  www.ngeorgia.com/parks/
  tallulah.html

• **Fort Mountain State Park**
  181 Fort Mountain Park Road
  Chatsworth, GA 30534
  706-695-2621
  www.ngeorgia.com/parks/
  fort.html

• **Moccasin Creek State Park**
  Rt. 1 Box 1634
  Clarkesville, GA 30523
  706-947-3194
  www.ngeorgia.com/parks/
  moccasin.html

CHATTAHOOCHEE NATIONAL FOREST CAMPING

There are a good number of Forest Service recreation areas located within the Chatta-hoochee National Forest. Each has campsites with picnic tables and many have drinking water and restroom facilities. These are open from late May through early September and sites may be taken on a first-come, first-served basis. A small fee is charged.

If roughing it is more your style, you may camp anywhere in the national forest that is not posted "no camping." No fee or permit is required. There are many primitive campsites along the forest roads, as well.

NORTHWEST GEORGIA

- **The Pocket**
  located between Dalton and Rome on Pocket Road

THE COHUTTAS & GA 515 CORRIDOR

- **Bear Creek**
  located at Lower
  Bear Creek Trailhead

- **Lake Conasauga**
  located on FS 68, east of Crandall
  (difficult to get to)

BULL MOUNTAIN AREA

- **Cooper Creek**
  located off GA 60 in
  Cooper Creek Scenic Area
  north of Suches

- **Desoto Falls**
  located on US 19/129,
  north of Dahlonega

- **Lake Winfield Scott**
  located on GA 180 between Vogel
  State Park and Suches

- **Waters Creek**
  located just north of
  Dahlonega on US 19

NORTHEAST GEORGIA

- **Lake Russell**
  located just east of Cornelia

- **Rabun Beach**
  located off US 441,
  south of Clayton

- **Andrews Cove**
  located on GA 17/75,
  north of Helen

SORBA

SORBA (the Southern Off-Road Bicycle Association) is a volunteer-run, nonprofit, officially chartered organization devoted to promoting land access, trail preservation and maintenance, and new trail building, so as to enhance mountain bike touring, racing, and fellowship for all Southeastern cyclists. It publishes the "Fat Tire Times" and issues land access alerts and other news to keep members informed of important topics, organized rides, work parties, races, socials, regional festivals, and other events. Every spring it holds its well-regarded Southeastern Mountain Bike Festival. SORBA membership entitles you to merchandise discounts, a "Fat Tire Times" subscription, web and email communications, volunteering, teaching, friendship, fellowship, enjoyment, and camaraderie. You're invited to join.

SORBA Membership Application

PERSONAL INFO
(Please Print)

Name_____DOB_____Gender_____

Adress_____

City_____State_____Zip_____

Home phone_____Work phone_____

Email address_____

I'm a new member [ ]. I learned about SORBA from_____

Family member #2 name_____Gender_____

My tax deductable Land Access Fund Donation is $_____

VOLUNTEERS ARE THE LIFEBLOOD OF OUR MTB ASSOCIATION. IT IS
EXTREMELY IMPORTANT FOR ALL MEMBERS TO DONATE A FEW HOURS
EACH QUARTER TO ONE OR MORE OF THE ACTIVITIES LISTED JUST
BELOW. TELL US WHAT YOU WANT TO DO.

[ ] Trail Maintenance   [ ] "Fat Tire Times" Production   [ ] Festival/Race Volunteer
[ ] Member Activities   [ ] Leading Organized Rides   [ ] Mountain Bike Patrol

CHAPTER

Athens [ ]
Atlanta [ ]
Augusta [ ]
Augusta (CSRA) [ ]
Charleston, SC (CHORBA) [ ]
Chattanooga, Tn [ ]
Ellijay [ ]
Gainesville [ ]
Habersham (UCCC) [ ]
Macon (OMBA) [ ]
NE Georgia [ ]
Roswell/Alph. (RAMBO) [ ]
Sumner Cty Cycle Club (TN) [ ]
Woodstock [ ]
At Large [ ]

MEMBERSHIP

Above & Beyond $1000 [ ]
Trail Builder $500 [ ]
Benefactor $250 [ ]
Fat Tire $100 [ ]
Corp. & Bike Shops $75 [ ]
Supporting Ind. $40 [ ]
Basic Individual $20 [ ]
Family $30 [ ]
IMBA membership add-on
for Ind. or Family $10 [ ]

(Make checks payable to SORBA)
Please mail this form and payment to:
SORBA • PO Box 1358, Gainesville, GA 30503

Current members, please check here ___ if you have
changed your address or other data.

Mountain biking is a rigorous
potentially dangerous sport, the
practice of which can result in
serious. life threating injuries. In
consideration of my membership,
I agree not to hold the Southern
Off-Road Bicycle Association
(SORBA), or any of its members
and/or directors liable for any in-
jury or damage, however caused,
which may result from my partici-
pation in any race or event of any
sort sponsored by or linked to
SORBA and/or it affiliates.

Signature:

_____

Date:_____
Parent/Guardian:

_____

Notes

Notes

Milestone Press
Outdoor Adventure Guides

MOUNTAIN BIKE SERIES

OFF THE BEATEN TRACK
by Jim Parham
• Vol. I: WNC—The Smokies
• Vol. II: WNC—Pisgah
• Vol. III: North Georgia
• Vol. IV: East Tennessee
• Vol. V: Northern Virginia
• Vol. VI: WV—Northern Highlands

• Tsali Mountain Bike Trails Map
• Bull Mountain Bike Trails Map

ROAD BIKE SERIES

• Road Bike Asheville, NC:
  Favorite Rides of the Blue Ridge
  Bicycle Club
  by The Blue Ridge Bicycle Club

• Road Bike the Smokies:
  16 Great Rides in North Carolina's
  Great Smoky Mountains
  by Jim Parham

• Road Bike North Georgia:
  25 Great Rides in the Mountains
  and Valleys of North Georgia
  by Jim Parham

PLAYBOATING

• A Playboater's Guide to the
  Ocoee River
• Playboating the Nantahala River:
  An Entry Level Guide
  by Kelly Fischer

ADVENTURE SERIES

• Natural Adventures in the
  Mountains of Western NC
• Natural Adventures in the
  Mountains of North Georgia
  by Mary Ellen Hammond
  & Jim Parham

MOTORCYCLE SERIES

• Motorcycle Adventures in the
  Southern Appalachians—
  North GA, East TN, Western NC
• Motorcycle Adventures in the
  Southern Appalachians—
  Asheville NC, Blue Ridge Pkwy,
  NC High Country
  by Hawk Hagebak

A NOTE TO THE READER

Can't find the Milestone Press book you want at a bookseller, bike shop or outfitter store near you? Don't despair—you can order it directly from us. Write: Milestone Press, PO Box 158, Almond, NC 28702; call us at 828-488-6601; or dial us up and shop on line at www.milestonepress.com.

We welcome your comments and suggestions regarding the contents of this book. Please write us at the address above or e-mail us at: otbt2@milestonepress.com.